Sandra Lumpkin
August 2000
Day after Susan & I returned
from Paris/Prague

W9-BXZ-943

Sunday Dinner

Sunday Dinner

SEASONAL MENUS TO ENJOY WITH FAMILY AND FRIENDS

by BARBARA SCOTT-GOODMAN
with MARY GOODBODY

illustrations by ROBBIN GOURLEY

CHRONICLE BOOKS
SAN FRANCISCO

*The authors would like to thank our editors Leslie Jonath and Sarah Putman
and designer Anne Galperin at Chronicle Books;
Deborah Callan for recipe testing; and agent Bob Cornfield.*

*We also thank our friends and families who happily ate Sunday dinners
on all days of the week while we were working on this book.*

Library of Congress Cataloging-in-Publication Data:

Scott-Goodman, Barbara.
Sunday dinner: seasonal menus to enjoy with friends and family/
by Barbara Scott-Goodman and Mary Goodbody.
p. cm.
Includes index.
ISBN 0-8118-1787-3 (hc)

1. Cookery. 2. Menus I. Goodbody, Mary. II. Title.
TX714. C3923 1998
642'.4—dc21 98-10825
CIP

Printed in Hong Kong
Book Design: Barbara Scott-Goodman

Distributed in Canada by Raincoast Books
8680 Cambie Street
Vancouver, British Columbia V6P 6M9

10 9 8 7 6 5 4 3 2 1

Chronicle Books
85 Second Street
San Francisco, California 94105

Web Site: www.chroniclebooks.com

Contents

INTRODUCTION

Regardless of how you spend the day, Sunday retains a pace and feeling all its own. Sunday can never be mistaken for Saturday or, thankfully, Monday. It is a day when time seems a little slower, when contemplation is a little easier, and when thoughts of family and friends come a little more readily.

Memories of Sunday dinners at our grandparents' houses may be warm and happy—or not—but the idea of the family gathering on Sunday afternoons to share a common meal has universal appeal. It signifies a willingness to slow down, to visit leisurely with those we most care about, while sharing a meal with folks from every generation. This is a time to create the gentle memories that carry us through the years and that, unbidden, support us as we go.

Sunday dinner at the close of this century is very different from the ritual that opened it. No longer is the meal centered around the requisite roast and potatoes; it is lighter and more contemporary but still retains the hallmark of simple American home

cooking. The menus we have assembled for each season reflect how we cook today with fresh, seasonal ingredients, and flavors and techniques culled from other cultures. This is updated familiar fare prepared simply and honestly and with ample room for extras such as savory sauces, full-bodied soups and homemade desserts.

For many of us, the weekend is the only time when we can indulge in the luxury of spending a few hours in the kitchen, which is why Sunday dinner reflects a spirit of generosity not always possible on more hectic weekdays. We can prepare an entire meal from start to finish without relying on the local take-out store or the frozen food case at the supermarket.

And there are advantages to serving dinner at two or three o'clock in the afternoon. It frees the morning for browsing in farmers markets, chopping vegetables, rolling pie crust—or letting a pot simmer on the back burner while you enjoy a cup of coffee and the newspaper. If you spend your weekends in the country or at the beach, it is a lovely finish to the idyll and allows guests to leave in plenty of time to get home (with stomachs full enough to render supper optional). It gives people time to spend Sunday morning as they prefer, whether that involves church, tennis, a trip to the flea market, household chores, a bike ride with the children or a lazy morning around the house.

Sunday dinner is a focused meal, unlike brunch, which is a muddle of breakfast and lunch and something of a puzzle to early risers, who prefer their cereal and orange juice when the day begins. This is a full-fledged meal with a main course, side dishes and dessert. It is a relaxed, celebratory meal for families to enjoy with each other and their friends.

In the spirit of a celebration, Sunday dinner lends itself to a well-set table. Now is your opportunity to use the damask tablecloth you found in the attic, to polish Grandma's silver candlesticks and arrange fresh flowers in that assortment of flea market vases. Paired with white bistro china and plain stemware, touches like these give your table a whimsical elegance that reflects your personal style. Or, your style might be bright placemats on the glass-top table on the deck, or your wedding china and crystal goblets reflected in the high gloss of a walnut table. Whichever route you choose, the lovingly set table says how much you care.

While none of the dishes on these pages is difficult to prepare, some do require time and a little planning. Most can be prepared ahead of time, which eliminates last-minute frenzy. The menus are divided by season, highlighting the produce available at its peak of freshness and flavor. We understand that many fruits and vegetables are available most of the year, but their higher price all too often goes beyond dollars and cents to reflect a deficit in flavor and texture. Nevertheless, if your heart is set on the Rhubarb Crisp and you cannot find fresh fruit, substitute frozen. If you crave the Roasted Acorn Squash Soup in mid-March when squash is scarce, use the squashes sold in specialty markets. The Red Pepper Ratatouille will never taste as delicious as it does on a summer afternoon, nor will the Cream of Watercress Soup taste as fresh as it does in the early spring or the Red Bartlett Pear Tart as luscious as on a crisp autumn day.

Because Sunday dinner requires time in the kitchen, we have devised the recipes with the rest of the week in mind. Many can be extended to serve as meals or parts of meals later in the week, when the workaday world impinges on the time we can devote to meal preparation. Included with each menu is a section called Pantry Suggestions, which highlights those recipes that can be increased, doubled, partially prepared or otherwise utilized when making mid-week meals. The suggestions may be for quick pasta suppers, light dishes to serve alongside broiled fish or chicken, or ideas for easy desserts or satisfying bag lunches. The Pantry Suggestions are just that: suggestions. Use them for inspiration or follow them literally. Planning a Sunday dinner with an eye for future meals is a good way to cook—efficient and stress-reducing. You can begin the week with the pleasant memory of Sunday's gathering coupled with the comforting knowledge that at least a few of the week's upcoming meals are planned.

We organized these menus using newly developed recipes as well as some we found in dog-eared files, or got from friends and neighbors and that over the years have made our own by adding personal touches, flavors and modern sensibilities. We hope they will become part of your family's weekend tradition, when you and your loved ones gather around the Sunday table to review the week, look forward to the coming days, laugh, talk and share what is good about being together with those you love.

SPRING DINNERS

He may live without books—what is knowledge but grieving?
He may live without hope—what is hope but deceiving?
He may live without love—what is passion but pining?
But where is the man who can live without dining?

OWEN MEREDITH
1831–1891

A Festive Spring Dinner

MENU

ROASTED PORK
TENDERLOIN WITH
ORANGE-CHILE GLAZE

ROASTED YAMS
AND RED ONIONS

LEMON
HARICOTS VERTS
AND CORN SALAD

RHUBARB CRISP

ROASTED PORK TENDERLOIN WITH ORANGE-CHILE GLAZE

Here is a spicy twist on traditional pork roast, sure to enliven a springtime meal. When paired with Roasted Yams and Red Onions, it makes a satisfying feast.

One 4- to 5-pound center-cut pork loin (see Note)
Salt and freshly ground black pepper

ORANGE-CHILE GLAZE:
2 tablespoons chili powder
1 tablespoon ground cumin
1 tablespoon ground coriander
$1/2$ tablespoon ground cinnamon
Juice of 2 oranges (about 1 cup)
$1/2$ cup cider vinegar
2 tablespoons finely chopped serrano or poblano chile
1 cup sugar
$1/4$ cup molasses

1. Preheat the oven to 350°F.

2. Put the pork loin on a rack in a shallow roasting pan and sprinkle lightly with salt and generously with pepper. Roast for 1 hour.

3. To prepare the glaze, in a saucepan, combine the chili powder, cumin, coriander and cinnamon and toast over medium heat for 2 or 3 minutes, stirring constantly, until the spices begin to smoke and become fragrant. Immediately remove from the heat.

4. Add the orange juice, vinegar, chiles, sugar and molasses, stir well and return to the heat. Bring to a boil, reduce the heat and simmer for about 45 minutes, stirring occasionally until thickened.

5. Remove the roast from the oven and spoon the pan drippings over the meat. Brush the glaze generously over the pork. Insert a meat thermometer into the thickest part of the pork and roast for 45 to 60 minutes longer, basting with the glaze, until the thermometer registers 160°F. Let the meat rest for 15 minutes. Cut into ½-inch-thick slices and serve hot.

Note: Ask the butcher to trim the loin and tie it with butcher twine.

Serves 6

ROASTED YAMS AND RED ONIONS

Take advantage of yams at all times of the year—not just during the winter holidays. Now, in the springtime, they are a lovely counterpoint to the green bean salad and boldly flavored pork roast. And the preparation is minimal—just slice them and roast for an hour or two.

6 yams, peeled and cut into $1/2$-inch dice
4 red onions, peeled and quartered
2 or 3 tablespoons olive oil
Salt and freshly ground black pepper, to taste

1. Preheat the oven to 350°F.
2. Arrange the yams and onions in an aluminum foil-lined roasting pan and sprinkle with olive oil, shaking the pan to coat them evenly. Season to taste with salt and pepper. Roast for $1\frac{1}{2}$ to 2 hours, stirring occasionally, until very tender. Serve immediately.

Serves 6

LEMON HARICOTS VERTS AND CORN SALAD

This knockout side dish makes delicious use of haricots verts, those thin French string beans in the markets in springtime. The fresh corn and basil add a taste of the summer soon to come.

2 pounds fresh haricots verts (green beans), rinsed and trimmed
3 ears fresh corn, husked
2 tablespoons finely chopped fresh basil
2 tablespoons finely chopped flat-leaf parsley
Juice of $1/2$ lemon
$1/3$ cup extra-virgin olive oil
1 tablespoon balsamic vinegar
Salt and freshly ground black pepper, to taste
$1/4$ cup pitted and halved kalamata olives

1. In a saucepan of boiling salted water, cook the beans for 4 or 5 minutes until crisp-tender. Rinse under cold running water and drain. Transfer to a bowl and set aside.
2. In a saucepan of boiling salted water, cook the ears of corn for 3 minutes. Rinse under cold running water and drain. When cool enough to handle, use a small sharp knife to scrape the kernels into the bowl with the beans. Hold the ears upright in the bowl or on a plate and scrape downward. Let the milky corn liquid mingle with the kernels and beans. Add the basil and parsley, sprinkle with the lemon juice and toss.
3. In a small bowl, whisk together the oil and vinegar and season to taste with salt and pepper. Pour over the salad and toss thoroughly.
4. Place on a serving platter or in a shallow bowl and top with the olive halves. Serve warm, chilled, or at room temperature.

Serves 6

PANTRY SUGGESTIONS

Roasted Pork Tenderloin with Orange-Chile Glaze—the glaze keeps for up to 2 weeks covered and refrigerated and can be used to glaze pork chops, chicken or full-flavored, firm fish such as tuna and swordfish. Use leftover pork in sandwiches made on country-style bread with grainy mustard and sliced onions or with a spoonful of coleslaw sandwiched with the pork.

Lemon Haricots Verts and Corn Salad—use leftovers tossed with salad greens and a light vinaigrette to add interest to a weekday green salad.

Rhubarb Crisp—turn the tables on this dessert by using it as a sauce spooned over vanilla, strawberry or coffee ice cream or frozen yogurt later in the week.

RHUBARB CRISP

Rhubarb is a spring fruit that is often paired with its seasonal partner, strawberries. This sweet, delicious crisp relies on tart rhubarb alone and is topped with a crumbly mixture of oats and nuts.

FILLING:
2 pounds fresh rhubarb, cubed (about 8 cups)
1 cup sugar
$1/4$ cup water
$1/2$ teaspoon ground cinnamon

TOPPING:
$1/2$ cup old-fashioned rolled oats
$1/3$ cup unbleached all-purpose flour
2 tablespoons light brown sugar
2 tablespoons chopped walnuts
1 teaspoon ground cinnamon
$1/4$ teaspoon freshly grated nutmeg
Pinch of baking powder
Pinch of salt
3 tablespoons chilled unsalted butter, cut into cubes

1. Preheat the oven to 350°F.
2. To prepare the filling, in a shallow, nonreactive saucepan, combine the rhubarb, sugar, water and cinnamon and cook over medium heat for about 15 minutes, stirring occasionally, until the mixture is thickened and the rhubarb is softened. Set aside to cool slightly.
3. To prepare the topping, combine the oats, flour, sugar, walnuts, cinnamon, nutmeg, baking powder, salt and butter in the bowl of a food processor and process for about 40 seconds until crumbly.
4. Spoon the rhubarb into a shallow 2-quart casserole and sprinkle the oat mixture evenly over the fruit. Bake for 35 to 40 minutes or until the topping is browned and the fruit is bubbling hot. Serve warm.

Serves 6

An Informal Seafood Dinner

SALAD OF SAUTÉED PEPPERS, ONIONS AND SUGAR SNAP PEAS WITH SESAME VINAIGRETTE

Mixing lightly cooked and raw vegetables yields salads with a splendid range of tastes and textures. In this salad, sautéed red and yellow peppers and red onions combined with peppery arugula make a flavorful statement, particularly when served in the same meal as a filling yet mild fish soup.

VEGETABLES:
2 tablespoons olive oil
2 red onions, sliced into rounds
1 red bell pepper, seeded and cut into thin strips
1 yellow bell pepper, seeded and cut into thin strips
1 pound sugar snap peas, trimmed
$^{1}/_{3}$ cup sesame seeds, lightly toasted (see Note)

VINAIGRETTE:
1 tablespoon balsamic vinegar
1 tablespoon rice vinegar
$^{1}/_{2}$ cup extra-virgin olive oil
Salt and freshly ground black pepper, to taste
2 bunches arugula, stemmed

1. To prepare the vegetables, in a large skillet or sauté pan, heat the oil over medium heat. Add the onions and sauté for about 3 minutes, until barely softened. Add the red and yellow peppers and sauté for 3 minutes longer. Reduce the heat to medium low, cover and cook for about 10 minutes longer or until the peppers are softened.
2. Raise the heat to medium and add the sugar snap peas and cook for about 2 minutes, stirring, until just tender. Stir in half of the sesame seeds and set aside.

MENU

SALAD OF SAUTÉED PEPPERS, ONIONS AND SUGAR SNAP PEAS WITH SESAME VINAIGRETTE

FISH SOUP WITH RED SNAPPER AND NEW POTATOES

WHOLE-WHEAT DINNER ROLLS WITH BASIL BUTTER

BLOOD ORANGE COMPOTE WITH GINGER COOKIES

3. To prepare the vinaigrette, in a small bowl, mix together the balsamic and rice vinegars. Slowly add the olive oil, pouring it in a steady stream while whisking constantly to emulsify the vinaigrette. Season to taste with salt and pepper. Set aside until ready to use.

4. In a large bowl, toss the arugula with half of the vinaigrette and arrange on 6 salad plates. Add the remaining vinaigrette to the onions, peppers and snap peas in the sauté pan and toss gently. Spoon on top of the arugula and sprinkle with the remaining sesame seeds and serve.

Note: To toast the sesame seeds, spread them in a small skillet and cook over medium heat, shaking the pan constantly, for 2 or 3 minutes or until fragrant and lightly browned. Transfer to a plate to cool and halt the cooking.

Serves 6

FISH SOUP WITH RED SNAPPER AND NEW POTATOES

When you add potatoes to fish soup, it becomes hearty enough to stand on its own as a main course for an early spring Sunday dinner. Any potatoes work, but tiny red new potatoes are especially wonderful. Snapper is a great fish for soup since it's firm enough to hold up in the broth and its bones make a savory stock. Other good choices are pompano and sea bass.

STOCK:

Bones, heads and tails from 1 large or 2 small red snappers (see Note)
1 carrot, quartered
1 onion, quartered
2 ribs celery, halved crosswise
1 tomato, peeled and chopped
1 cup dry white wine
$1/2$ teaspoon dried tarragon
$1/4$ teaspoon dried thyme
6 sprigs flat-leaf parsley
Salt and freshly ground black pepper, to taste

SOUP:

2 tablespoons olive oil
1 large yellow onion, finely chopped
1 red pepper, seeded and finely chopped
1 can (28 ounces) plum tomatoes, with liquid
Pinch of saffron powder or threads
1 pound small red new potatoes, cut into $1/2$-inch dice
4 red snapper fillets (about $1^1/2$ pounds total), cut into large chunks
Salt and freshly ground black pepper, to taste
Juice of $1/2$ lemon
Chopped flat-leaf parsley, for garnish

1. To prepare the stock, put the fish bones, heads and tails in a stock-pot and add enough water to cover by several inches (about 3 quarts). Add the carrot, onion, celery, tomato, wine, tarragon, thyme and parsley and bring to a boil over high heat. Season with salt and pepper to taste, reduce the heat and simmer, uncovered, for $1\frac{1}{2}$ hours, skimming and discarding any foam that rises to the top.

2. Strain the stock into a bowl through a dampened cheesecloth draped over a large sieve. Cool, cover and refrigerate. (At this point the stock may be refrigerated for 1 day or frozen for up to 2 weeks.)

3. To prepare the soup, in a stockpot, heat the oil over medium-high heat and sauté the onion for about 5 minutes until softened and golden. Add the red pepper and cook for about 5 minutes longer.

4. Add 6 cups of the fish stock, tomatoes and their juice and saffron. Bring to a boil, reduce the heat to medium low and simmer gently, covered for about 10 minutes, stirring occasionally to break up the tomatoes. Add the potatoes, bring the soup to a boil, reduce the heat to medium and simmer for about 20 minutes until the potatoes are fork-tender.

5. Raise the heat and bring the soup to a boil. Add the fish fillets, reduce the heat to medium high and cook for 5 or 6 minutes or until the fish is opaque and flakes when pierced with a fork. Season to taste with salt and pepper and stir in the lemon juice. Taste and correct the seasoning, if necessary.

6. Ladle into large soup bowls, garnish with parsley and serve.

Note: Ask the fishmonger to save the bones, heads and tails when filleting the snapper to use in the stock.

Serves 6

WHOLE-WHEAT DINNER ROLLS WITH BASIL BUTTER

Freshly baked dinner rolls turn a simple Sunday dinner into a particularly warm and welcoming one. Yeast breads should not be daunting. The dough is extremely forgiving and while it should not be left to rise for much more than the recommended time, it allows for plenty of time to attend to the rest of the meal. These are a special treat served warm with fresh basil butter.

ROLLS:
1 package active dry yeast ($^1/_4$ ounce)
$1^1/_4$ cups lukewarm water (105°F. to 115°F.)
2 tablespoons honey
1 teaspoon salt
1 tablespoon canola oil
$1^1/_4$ cups whole-wheat flour
$1^1/_2$ to 2 cups unbleached all-purpose flour

BUTTER:
1 cup (2 sticks) unsalted butter, softened
¼ cup finely chopped basil leaves
¼ teaspoon salt or more to taste

1. To prepare the rolls, in a large bowl, sprinkle the yeast over the water and set aside for about 10 minutes to bubble and foam. Add the honey, salt, oil, whole-wheat flour and ¾ cup of the all-purpose flour and stir with a wooden spoon to mix well.

2. Add the remaining all-purpose flour, 4 to 5 tablespoons at a time, stirring constantly, until the dough holds together and pulls away from the sides of the bowl. You may not need all the flour.

3. Turn the dough out onto a lightly floured surface and knead for 8 to 10 minutes, or until the dough is smooth and elastic. As you knead, add more flour if necessary.

4. Form the dough into a ball and transfer to a large buttered or oiled bowl, turning the dough to coat it on all sides with butter or oil. Cover loosely with a kitchen towel and set aside in a warm place to rise for about 45 minutes or until doubled in bulk.

5. Turn the dough out onto a lightly floured surface and knead briefly. Divide into 14 or 16 equal pieces and, using your hands, form each into a roll. Transfer the rolls to 2 lightly buttered baking sheets, leaving about 2 inches between each, and cover with kitchen towels. Set aside to rise for about 30 minutes in a warm place until nearly doubled in bulk.

6. Preheat the oven to 375°F. about 20 minutes before the end of the second rising.

7. Bake the rolls for 12 to 15 minutes or until the bottoms of the rolls sound hollow when tapped and the rolls are golden brown. Cool on wire racks.

8. To prepare the butter, in a small bowl, mash the butter with a fork. Add the basil and mash gently to mix. Season to taste with salt. Cover and refrigerate until ready to serve.

Makes 14 to 16 rolls; about 1 cup butter

BLOOD ORANGE COMPOTE

Blood oranges are so named because of the unusual red color of their flesh. The skins, too, sometimes have a rosy hue. The oranges are slightly tart and make a deliciously fresh-tasting compote to complete Sunday dinner. Serve them with spicy ginger cookies.

4 blood oranges (see Note)
¼ cup orange juice
2 tablespoons sugar
½ teaspoon ground cinnamon
1 teaspoon grated orange zest
¼ cup coarsely chopped walnuts
Three 2-inch-long strips orange zest, halved, for garnish
Fresh mint sprigs, for garnish

1. Peel the oranges and cut away the white pith. Holding the oranges over a bowl to catch the juices, cut the oranges into segments. Transfer the orange segments and the collected juices to a nonreactive saucepan. Add the orange juice, sugar and cinnamon and bring to a boil over medium-high heat, stirring gently.
2. Stir in the grated zest, reduce the heat and simmer for 6 or 7 minutes or until slightly thickened. Stir in the walnuts and remove from the heat. Set aside to cool. Serve immediately or cover and refrigerate for up to 2 days.
3. To serve, spoon the compote into small bowls and garnish with strips of zest and mint.

Note: Blood oranges are available in the spring, but if you cannot find them, use any sweet orange.

Serves 6

GINGER COOKIES

These cookies are as delicious served on their own as they are when served alongside the compote.

2 cups unbleached all-purpose flour
1½ teaspoons baking soda
½ teaspoon salt
1 tablespoon ground ginger
1½ teaspoons ground cinnamon
½ teaspoon ground cloves
1 cup sugar
¾ cup (1½ sticks) unsalted butter, softened
1 large egg
¼ cup dark molasses
Sugar, for rolling

1. Preheat the oven to 350°F. Lightly butter 2 baking sheets.
2. Combine the flour, baking soda, salt, ginger, cinnamon and cloves in a bowl and whisk 8 to 10 times.
3. In the bowl of an electric mixer set on medium speed, cream the sugar and butter. Add the egg and beat until fluffy. Add the molasses and beat to mix.
4. Add the dry ingredients to the batter and beat until smooth.
5. Spread sugar in a shallow dish.
6. Roll walnut-sized pieces of dough between lightly floured or greased palms into 1½ inch balls. Roll each ball in the sugar to coat, and transfer to the baking sheets, leaving about 1½ inches between the cookies. Bake for 10 to 12 minutes or until the cookies spread and the tops crack. Cool on wire racks.

Makes 30 to 34 large cookies

PANTRY SUGGESTIONS

Salad of Sautéed Peppers, Onions and Sugar Snap Peas with Sesame Vinaigrette—use the same blending of sautéed vegetables as a topping for broiled or grilled chicken or fish. Use the vinaigrette on a salad of buttery salad greens or blanched string beans.

Fish Soup with Red Snapper and New Potatoes—make twice the amount of stock and freeze it for soup later in the week or month. Use it as the base for clam chowder, following the recipe for fish soup but substituting the snapper with fresh shucked clams and adding a few more potatoes.

Whole-Wheat Dinner Rolls with Basil Butter—the dough for the rolls can be formed into a loaf and baked as bread. Use leftover rolls for sandwiches or split them and toast them for breakfast. The basil butter can be wrapped in plastic and foil and frozen for up to a month to use over steamed vegetables or broiled fish. Substitute parsley or another fresh herb for the basil and add garlic to give the butter a different flavor.

Blood Orange Compote—spoon the compote over pound cake for a simple dessert. It is also good spooned over oatmeal or cream of wheat for breakfast.

The Best of Springtime Dinner

MENU

CREAM OF
WATERCRESS SOUP

SALMON AND SPRING
VEGETABLES
BAKED IN PARCHMENT

ASPARAGUS WITH
FRESH CHIVE BUTTER

LEMON-GLAZED
TEA CAKE WITH
FRESH STRAWBERRIES

CREAM OF WATERCRESS SOUP

Watercress, which grows under crusty snow at winter's end, is a hopeful harbinger of early spring. The peppery cress tastes lovely and fresh when made into a creamy soup, but the potato-based broth is so versatile, the soup can be made with vegetables other than watercress. Try it with cooked asparagus, broccoli, cauliflower or carrots, too. And if the weather is balmy, serve it cold.

SOUP BASE:
2 tablespoons olive oil
1 tablespoon unsalted butter
1 leek, rinsed and diced (white and green part)
2 cups thinly sliced onions (about 4 onions)
4 cups chicken stock, preferably homemade
4 cups water
6 russet potatoes, peeled and diced

SOUP:
1 cup milk
2 cups rinsed, stemmed and finely chopped fresh watercress (about 2 bunches)
$1/2$ teaspoon ground nutmeg
Salt and freshly ground black pepper
3 tablespoons chopped flat-leaf parsley

1. To prepare the base, in a stockpot, heat the oil and butter over medium heat until the butter melts. Add the leek and onions and sauté for about 10 minutes, stirring occasionally, until tender. Add the stock, water and potatoes and bring to a boil over high heat. Reduce the heat to medium-low and simmer, covered, for 15 to 20 minutes, or until the potatoes are fork-tender. Cool for about 20 minutes.

2. Transfer the soup base to a food processor or blender and process until smooth. (This may have to be done in batches.)

3. Return the soup base to the pot, add the milk and heat over medium heat, stirring, until hot. Add the watercress and nutmeg and season to taste with salt and pepper. Add the parsley and serve immediately.

Note: To serve cold, let the soup cool for about 30 minutes. Cover and refrigerate until cold. The base alone will keep in the refrigerator for up to 3 days and in the freezer for up to 1 month.

Serves 6 to 8

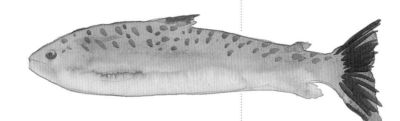

SALMON AND SPRING VEGETABLES BAKED IN PARCHMENT

Cooking fragile salmon fillets and fresh spring vegetables in parchment is remarkably fuss-free, and the presentation is truly special. The golden brown packets are served at the table as fragrant gifts for each person to open and eat directly from the wrapping. The food inside is moist and tender with lightly mingled fresh flavors—a taste of spring itself. The only secret to success is to use the freshest fish and vegetables available.

4 tablespoons extra-virgin olive oil
6 salmon fillets (about 2¼ pounds total)
2 zucchini, trimmed and julienned
1 large bulb fennel, trimmed and julienned
2 carrots, julienned
3 scallions, trimmed and sliced ¼-inch thick
2 tablespoons chopped fresh basil
Salt and freshly ground pepper to taste
6 lemon slices

1. Preheat the oven to 375°F. Cut 6 sheets of parchment paper, each measuring 18 by 12 inches. Fold each sheet in half so that it measures 9 by 12 inches. Open a parchment sheet and position it so that it resembles an open book. Brush the bottom half with oil, brushing over the fold.

2. Lay a salmon fillet on the oiled portion near the fold, centered between the top and bottom of the sheet. Arrange some zucchini, fennel and carrots alongside the fish and brush the top of the fish with more oil. Sprinkle scallions and basil over all. Season with salt and pepper and lay a lemon slice on top of each fillet. Repeat with the remaining sheets of parchment and ingredients.

3. Fold the parchment paper over the food and seal tightly by overlapping the edges, top and sides, to make secure packets. Transfer to 2 baking sheets without leaving much space between the packets. Bake for 10 to 12 minutes, depending on the thickness of the fillets.

4. Transfer each packet to a dinner plate and serve immediately. Take care when opening the packets; the escaping steam is hot.

Serves 6

ASPARAGUS WITH FRESH CHIVE BUTTER

Asparagus is an elegant vegetable that is especially plentiful and flavorful in the spring, its natural growing season. Indulge in it as often as possible, serving it with little embellishment alongside other springtime foods, such as salmon. Look for straight stalks with tightly closed and pointed tips.

3 pounds moderately slender fresh asparagus
4 tablespoons (½ stick) unsalted butter
2 tablespoons finely chopped shallots
1 teaspoon finely grated lemon zest
1 tablespoon fresh lemon juice
1 teaspoon salt
3 tablespoons finely snipped fresh chives
2 teaspoons finely chopped fresh mint leaves
Salt and freshly ground black pepper to taste

1. Cut or break off the tough woody ends of the asparagus stalks and discard. (Young asparagus may not have tough ends.) Using a vegetable peeler and starting just below the tip, peel the skin from each stalk.

2. In a large saucepan or skillet, bring enough lightly salted water to cover the asparagus to a boil over high heat. Add the asparagus, reduce the heat to simmer, and cook for 3 to 5 minutes, just until tender. Drain well.

3. In a saucepan, melt 1 tablespoon of butter over medium heat. Add the shallots and sauté for 2 to 3 minutes until transparent and softened. Add the remaining 3 tablespoons of butter and continue stirring the shallots and butter until the butter melts. Remove from the heat and stir in the lemon zest, lemon juice and salt. Stir in the chives and mint.

4. Transfer the asparagus to a shallow bowl and carefully toss with the butter. Season with salt and pepper and serve immediately.

Serves 6

27

Lemon-Glazed Tea Cake with Fresh Strawberries

Lemony cake topped with a sweet old-fashioned sugar glaze tastes as refreshing as a spring evening and is the perfect ending to this Sunday dinner. The recipe makes two cake loaves, which means there should be plenty left over to enjoy during the coming week. If your plans do not allow for this, wrap a cooled but unglazed cake in foil and freeze it for up to a month.

Cake:
2 1/2 cups unbleached all-purpose flour
1 teaspoon baking powder
5 large eggs
1 1/2 cups sugar
3/4 cup heavy cream
7 tablespoons unsalted butter, melted
2 tablespoons fresh lemon juice
Grated zest of 1 lemon

Lemon Glaze:
1 cup confectioners' sugar
Juice of 1 lemon

2 cups fresh strawberries, washed, hulled,
  and sliced

1. To prepare the cake, preheat the oven to 350°F. Butter two 8-by-5-inch loaf pans.
2. In a bowl, combine the flour and baking powder and whisk to mix.
3. In the bowl of an electric mixer, combine the eggs and sugar and beat on medium-high speed until smooth. Reduce the speed to low and slowly add the cream and the flour mixture, alternating additions and beginning and ending with the cream. Add the butter, lemon juice and zest and beat until mixed and smooth.

4. Pour the batter into the loaf pans, dividing it evenly and smoothing the top of each. Bake on the center rack for about 1 hour until the tops are golden brown, pull away slightly from the sides of the pan and a toothpick inserted in the center comes out clean. Cool in the pans set on wire racks for about 15 minutes before turning out to cool to room temperature on the wire racks.

5. To prepare the glaze, combine the confectioners' sugar and lemon juice in a bowl and whisk well.

6. Set the racks holding the cakes on wax paper and pour the glaze over the cakes, letting it run down the sides. Slice the cake and serve each slice topped with strawberries.

Makes 2 loaf cakes; serves 8 to 12

PANTRY SUGGESTIONS

Cream of Watercress Soup—make enough soup base for other soups, which may be served hot or cold. Make Cream of Asparagus, Broccoli, Spinach or Carrot soup by adding cooked vegetables to the soup base. Add cooked leeks and make vichyssoise. Or make double the amount of Cream of Watercress Soup and refrigerate it for a simple supper or lunch at home later in the week.

Asparagus with Fresh Chive Butter—make extra chive butter and refrigerate it so that it hardens. Spread it on sliced baguettes and top with capers or sliced olives to serve with drinks later in the week or as a snack. Try tossing boiled potatoes or egg noodles with chive butter, or use it to top baked potatoes.

Lemon-Glazed Tea Cake with Fresh Strawberries—the recipe makes enough cake batter for 2 loaf cakes. Cut the leftover cake into slices and serve it toasted and spread with preserves or jam as an accompaniment for tea. Serve it topped with citrus sorbet or raspberry sauce for a midweek dessert. Just plain, the cake is great for school or work lunch sacks.

SUMMER DINNERS

They dined on mince, and slices of quince,
Which they ate with a runcible spoon;
And hand in hand, on the edge of the sand,
They danced by the light of the moon.

EDWARD LEAR
1812–1888

A Summer Weekend Barbecue

∾

YELLOW TOMATO SALSA

Some like it hot, and if you make this salsa a day or two ahead of time, it will become hotter and more intense. But if you prefer a milder salsa, use the fresh chiles sparingly and make the salsa the day you plan to serve it. Serve with blue and yellow tortilla chips.

3 ears fresh corn, husked
4 yellow tomatoes, cut into $1/4$-inch dice
1 tablespoon finely chopped serrano or poblano chile
$1/4$ cup finely chopped fresh parsley
2 tablespoons minced fresh chives
Juice of 1 lime (about $1/4$ cup)
$1/4$ cup tomato juice
2 teaspoons sugar
Salt and freshly ground black pepper, to taste

1. Bring a large pot of lightly salted water to a boil over high heat and cook the corn for 3 minutes. Drain and rinse under cold running water to halt the cooking. When cool enough to handle, using a sharp knife, scrape the kernels off the cobs and transfer them to a bowl. Hold the ears upright in the bowl or on a plate and scrape downward. Let the milky corn liquid mingle with the kernels.
2. Add the tomatoes, chiles, parsley and chives and toss well. Add the lime juice, tomato juice and sugar, season with salt and pepper and toss well. Taste and adjust the seasonings. Cover and refrigerate for at least 1 hour and for no longer than 2 hours before serving.

Serves 6; makes about 2 cups

CITRUS-GRILLED CHICKEN THIGHS

Here's a summertime grilling recipe bursting with sunny citrusy flavors that is nearly as good cooked indoors under the broiler. When grilling dark meat, we find it helpful to precook the chicken for about 15 minutes in the oven to prevent drying or charring.

Juice of 2 limes (about 1/2 cup)
1/3 cup orange juice
1/4 cup olive oil
2 cloves garlic, thinly sliced
Salt and freshly ground black pepper, to taste
12 chicken thighs

1. To make the marinade, whisk together the lime juice, orange juice and olive oil. Add the garlic cloves and season with salt and pepper.
2. Lay the chicken thighs in a large aluminum foil–lined roasting pan. Pour the marinade over the chicken, cover and refrigerate for 1 hour.
3. Preheat the oven to 350° F. Prepare a charcoal or gas grill or preheat the broiler (see Note).
4. Bake the chicken for 15 minutes, remove from the oven and set aside. When the coals are covered with white ash or the grill or broiler is medium hot, lift the chicken from the pan and reserve the marinade. Grill or broil the chicken, turning frequently, for 15 to 20 minutes, until the juices run clear when the meat is pierced with a knife.
5. Pour the marinade into a saucepan and bring to a boil over medium-high heat. Cook for about 1 minute and then keep warm.
6. To serve, arrange the chicken thighs on a large platter and drizzle with the marinade.

Note: If broiling the chicken, it may be easier to skip the baking and cook it entirely in the broiler, particularly if the broiler is built into the oven. To broil without prebaking, turn the chicken thighs every 10 minutes, broiling for a total of 25 to 30 minutes.

Serves 6

Black Bean Salad with Toasted Cumin Vinaigrette

Deep and rich looking, black bean salad is a lovely warm-weather dish to serve with this menu. There is no point not making a lot of the salad, as it keeps for days and you'll want to keep tasting all week long.

Beans:
4 cups (28 ounces) dried black beans
4 cups chicken stock, preferably homemade
4 cups water
1 red bell pepper, seeded, deveined, and cut into $1/4$-inch dice
6 scallions (white and green parts), trimmed and cut into $1/2$-inch pieces
1 red onion, thinly sliced
$1/2$ cup finely chopped cilantro or flat-leaf parsley
Juice of $1/2$ lemon
Salt and freshly ground black pepper

Vinaigrette:
1 tablespoon ground cumin
1 tablespoon chili powder
2 tablespoons balsamic vinegar
$2/3$ cup extra-virgin olive oil

1. To prepare the beans, pick them over, discarding any broken or misshapen ones, and rinse thoroughly. Put the beans in a large bowl, add enough cold water to cover by about 2 inches and set aside to soak for 6 to 8 hours or overnight.

2. Drain the beans and transfer them to a stockpot. Add the stock and water and bring to a boil over high heat. Reduce the heat and simmer the beans, uncovered, for 40 to 50 minutes until just tender, skimming any foam that rises to the surface. Be careful not to overcook. You should be able to mash a bean against the roof of your mouth but it should retain its general shape. Drain the beans, rinse under cold running water and set aside to cool.

3. Meanwhile, combine the red pepper, scallions, onion and cilantro in a large bowl. Add the lemon juice, season with salt and pepper and toss gently.

4. To prepare the vinaigrette, put the cumin and chili powder in a small skillet and toast over medium heat for 2 or 3 minutes, stirring constantly, just until they begin to smoke. Immediately remove the skillet from the heat.

5. In a small bowl, whisk the vinegar and olive oil together until thickened. Add the toasted spices and whisk again.

6. To assemble the salad, add the cooled beans to the vegetable mixture and toss to mix. Pour the vinaigrette over the salad and toss gently. Set aside at room temperature for at least 1 hour to give the flavors time to blend. Or cover and refrigerate for up to 12 hours. Serve chilled or at room temperature.

Serves 10 to 12

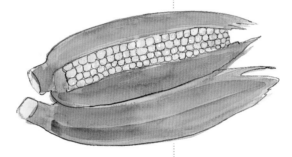

Tomato, Avocado and Corn Salad

Keeping it simple is what summer is all about, and this colorful salad is nothing if not simple. Without question, the joys of summer include juicy, full-flavored tomatoes and tender corn; this salad takes glorious advantage of them. Look for the ripest tomatoes, avocados that are just soft to the touch, and sweet corn that has been picked only hours earlier.

2 red onions, cut into 1/4-inch-thick rings
1 to 2 tablespoons olive oil
3 ears fresh corn, husked
4 to 6 tomatoes, cut into 1/2-inch dice
3 ripe avocados, peeled, pitted, and cut into 1/2-inch dice
1/4 cup finely chopped flat-leaf parsley
1 tablespoon balsamic vinegar
2 tablespoons extra-virgin olive oil
Salt and freshly ground black pepper, to taste

1. Preheat the oven to 350°F.
2. Lay the onion rings in a roasting pan and sprinkle with the olive oil, tossing gently to mix. Bake for about 45 minutes, until tender. Shake the pan occasionally to keep the onions evenly coated and to prevent burning. Set aside to cool.
3. Meanwhile, bring a large pot of lightly salted water to a boil over high heat and cook the corn for 3 minutes. Drain and rinse under cold, running water to halt the cooking. When cool enough to handle, scrape the kernels off the cobs and transfer them to a bowl. Add the roasted onions, tomatoes, avocados and parsley and toss gently. Add the vinegar and oil, season with salt and pepper and toss gently. Taste and adjust the seasonings. Serve immediately or cover and refrigerate until ready to serve.

Serves 6

PEACH-RASPBERRY COBBLER

Peaches and raspberries speak of high summer when a simple fruit dessert is called for to end the meal. This one is made with a dough that is quickly mixed in a food processor before it is rolled, pressed into a baking dish and filled with the luscious fruit.

DOUGH:
1½ cups sifted unbleached all-purpose flour
¼ teaspoon salt
5 tablespoons unsalted butter, chilled
¼ cup vegetable shortening, chilled
4 or 5 tablespoons ice water

FILLING:
6 ripe peaches, peeled, pitted and thinly sliced
  (approximately 2½ pounds)
1 cup fresh raspberries
½ cup sugar
3 tablespoons unsalted butter, cut into pieces

Whipped cream or ice cream, for garnish (optional)

1. Preheat the oven to 450°F. Lightly butter a 7-by-9-inch baking dish.
2. To make the dough, combine the flour, salt, butter and shortening in the bowl of a food processor fitted with a metal blade and pulse until the mixture resembles coarse meal. Slowly add the ice water, a tablespoon or two at a time, and process until the dough begins to hold together and gathers on the blade. Shape the dough into a ball, working in a little more flour if necessary. Wrap in waxed paper and refrigerate for 30 to 60 minutes.
3. To prepare the filling, put the peaches and raspberries in a large bowl. Sprinkle the sugar over the fruit and toss together. Set aside at room temperature for about 15 minutes to give juices time to accumulate and sweeten.

PANTRY SUGGESTIONS

Yellow Tomato Salsa—the salsa keeps for up to 5 days and can be served later in the week spooned over grilled swordfish or tuna, chicken, steak or pork chops. It adds zip to salads and sandwiches, too.

Citrus-Grilled Chicken Thighs—leftovers can be tossed with pasta and vegetables, used to make classic chicken salad or added to green salads. Left intact, the cold chicken is delicious served with leftover Yellow Tomato Salsa.

Black Bean Salad with Toasted Cumin Vinaigrette—the recipe makes more than you will need for one meal so plan to serve this later in the week with grilled or broiled fish or beef. It can stand on its own as the main course of a light lunch or quick supper.

Peach-Raspberry Cobbler—if there are any leftovers (which is doubtful!), serve them spooned over ice cream or frozen yogurt.

4. On a lightly floured surface or on a piece of waxed paper and using a floured rolling pin, roll the dough into a rough 10-by-12-inch rectangle. Line the baking dish with the dough, allowing the excess to hang over the sides. Spoon the peach and raspberry mixture evenly over the dough and dot it with butter. Fold the overhanging dough back over the fruit. It will not cover the fruit but will form a decorative edge.

5. Put the cobbler on a center rack of the oven and immediately reduce the temperature to 425°F. Bake for 35 to 45 minutes, or until the crust is golden and the fruit is bubbling hot.

6. To serve, spoon the cobbler, warm or at room temperature, into bowls. Serve with whipped cream or ice cream, if desired.

Serves 6 to 8

An Elegant Meal From the Grill

WHITE BEAN AND BASIL PURÉE WITH PEASANT BREAD TOASTS

The key to this easy appetizer is to use the best bread you can find. We like rosemary-scented peasant bread, but any freshly baked hearth bread works very nicely.

PURÉE:
1 cup (¹/₂ pound) dried white cannellini beans
2 onions
6 cups water
1 cup chicken stock, preferably homemade
6 sprigs fresh parsley
2 tablespoons olive oil
6 cloves garlic, halved
¹/₂ teaspoon dried oregano
¹/₄ teaspoon dried thyme
2 tablespoons chopped fresh basil
2 tablespoons crème fraîche
Juice of ¹/₂ lemon
Salt and freshly ground pepper, to taste

TOASTS:
3 tablespoons olive oil
12 round slices peasant bread (see Note)
6 kalamata olives, pitted and halved, for garnish
12 whole basil leaves, for garnish

1. To prepare the purée, pick over the beans, discarding any broken or misshapen ones, and rinse thoroughly. Put the beans in a large bowl, add enough cold water to cover by about 2 inches and set aside to soak for 6 to 8 hours or overnight.

MENU

WHITE BEAN AND BASIL PURÉE WITH PEASANT BREAD TOASTS

GRILLED BUTTERFLIED LEG OF LAMB WITH BALSAMIC VINEGAR AND FRESH HERB MARINADE

RED PEPPER RATATOUILLE

LEMON BASMATI RICE

OLD-FASHIONED LEMON PUDDING WITH SEASONAL BERRIES

39

2. Drain the beans and transfer them to a stockpot. Quarter 1 of the onions, reserving the other for a later use. Add the water, stock, quartered onion and parsley and bring to a boil over high heat. Reduce the heat and simmer the beans, uncovered, for 40 to 50 minutes until just tender, skimming any foam that rises to the surface. Be careful not to overcook. You should be able to mash a bean against the roof of your mouth but it should retain its general shape. Drain, discard the onions and parsley and set the beans aside.

3. Heat the olive oil in a large skillet. Chop the remaining onion, add it and the garlic to the skillet and cook over medium heat, stirring, for 10 to 15 minutes or until very tender. Add the drained beans, oregano, thyme and basil and cook over low heat, stirring, for 5 to 10 minutes, or until the beans are heated through. Set aside to cool.

4. Transfer the bean mixture to a food processor fitted with the metal blade. Add the crème fraîche and pulse 8 or 9 times or until smooth. Add the lemon juice and season to taste with salt and pepper. Pulse until smooth.

5. To prepare the toasts, preheat the oven to 350°F.

6. Brush the bread with the olive oil and lay on a baking sheet. Bake for about 15 minutes or until lightly browned.

7. To serve, spread the purée generously on the toasts and top each with olive halves and basil leaves for garnish.

Note: Peasant bread, also called hearth bread or country loaves, is sold in many specialty stores, bakeries and gourmet take-out shops. It is a free-form rounded loaf with a crisp crust and a soft, large-crumbed interior. If possible, buy the bread the day you plan to use it because it does not keep well, although it will freeze for up to a month.

Serves 6

GRILLED BUTTERFLIED LEG OF LAMB WITH BALSAMIC VINEGAR AND FRESH HERB MARINADE

A marinade of balsamic vinegar and red wine flavored with fresh garden herbs such as rosemary, oregano and mint gives this grilled leg of lamb a wonderfully aromatic quality. The lamb will yield more than six servings—but it makes delicious leftovers.

¼ cup balsamic vinegar
1 cup dry red wine
¼ cup olive oil
4 large cloves garlic, thinly sliced
1 tablespoon crushed fresh rosemary
1 teaspoon chopped fresh oregano
¼ cup chopped fresh mint
Freshly ground black pepper
One 4- to 5-pound butterflied leg of lamb (see Note)

1. Combine the vinegar, wine, olive oil, garlic, rosemary, oregano, mint and pepper and whisk to mix. Lay the lamb in a large shallow glass or ceramic baking dish, pour the marinade over it, cover and refrigerate for about 6 hours, turning the lamb occasionally.

2. Prepare a charcoal or gas grill until the coals are covered with white ash.

3. Lift the lamb from the marinade and reserve it. Grill the lamb 4 to 6 inches from the coals for about 40 minutes, basting frequently with the marinade and turning at least once. After 30 minutes, check the lamb for doneness every few minutes. Do not overcook.

4. Carve the lamb into thin slices and serve immediately.

Note: Butterflied leg of lamb is a leg with the bone removed so that the meat can be laid relatively flat for grilling or broiling. When buying the lamb, remind the butcher that the weight refers to the butterflied leg once the bone has been removed.

Serves 6

41

RED PEPPER RATATOUILLE

Summer wouldn't be the same without ratatouille. There are as many ways to make this vegetable melange as there are zucchini in the garden. In this version, we cook the eggplant and squash separately and then combine them with the softened onions, peppers and tomatoes for the final 25 minutes of cooking, a method that allows each vegetable to maintain its flavor integrity. If you have vine-ripened August tomatoes, substitute them for the canned plum tomatoes.

1 eggplant (about 1 pound)
1 zucchini (about 8 ounces)
1 crookneck squash (about 8 ounces)
1 tablespoon salt
5 tablespoons olive oil
1 small onion, thinly sliced
1 green bell pepper, seeded and thinly sliced
1 red bell pepper, seeded and thinly sliced
4 cloves garlic, finely minced
Salt and freshly ground black pepper, to taste
1 cup canned plum tomatoes (measured before draining)
   drained, and sliced into strips, or 1 cup chopped fresh tomatoes
   (about 2 tomatoes)
$1/4$ cup chopped fresh flat-leaf parsley

1. Peel the eggplant and cut lengthwise into strips about 2 inches long and ¼ inch thick. Peel the zucchini and squash and cut lengthwise into strips about 2 inches long and ⅜ inch thick. Transfer the vegetables to a bowl, add the tablespoon of salt, toss and let stand for 30 to 45 minutes. Drain the liquid that accumulates in the bowl and pat the vegetables dry using paper towels or a dishtowel.

2. In a large skillet, heat the olive oil over medium heat. Add the vegetables and sauté for about 10 minutes until lightly browned on both sides. Remove with a slotted spoon and transfer to a large stockpot.

3. Put the onion, bell peppers and garlic in the same skillet, adding a little more oil, if necessary. Season to taste with salt and pepper and

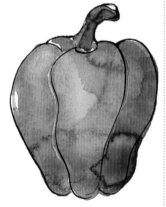

cook over medium-low heat for 10 to 15 minutes, stirring occasionally, until softened. Add the tomatoes, raise the heat to high and cook for about 10 minutes, stirring occasionally, until the mixture is bubbling. Stir in the parsley.

4. Add the tomato mixture to the eggplant mixture and stir gently. Set over low heat, cover, and simmer for about 15 minutes, stirring occasionally. Uncover, raise the heat to medium-high and bring the ratatouille to a gentle boil. Cook for about 10 minutes longer or until the mixture thickens. Adjust the seasonings and serve hot, warm or at room temperature.

Serves 6

LEMON BASMATI RICE

Basmati rice, with its distinctive nutlike flavor, is a tasty, quick side dish and is especially delicious when mixed with a bit of refreshing grated lemon zest.

2 cups uncooked basmati rice
3 1/2 cups water
1/2 teaspoon salt
1 tablespoon finely grated lemon zest

1. Combine the rice, water and salt in a 3-quart saucepan and bring to a boil over high heat. Stir once, reduce the heat, cover and simmer for 15 to 20 minutes or until the liquid is absorbed.
2. Remove from the heat. Stir in the lemon zest, cover and let stand for 5 minutes before serving.

Serves 6

PANTRY SUGGESTIONS

White Bean and Basil Purée with Peasant Bread Toasts—the purée is even better after a day or two in the refrigerator. Spread it on vegetable sandwiches, cold grilled meats or stir it into vegetable soups for flavor and thickening. And it's always delicious on crackers and bread.

Grilled Butterflied Leg of Lamb with Balsamic Vinegar and Fresh Herb Marinade—cold lamb is delicious thinly sliced and served in a sandwich, particularly if the sandwich is also made with cold ratatouille. Toss the cold meat with a curried vinaigrette, roasted red peppers, scallions and minced garlic for a main course salad.

Red Pepper Ratatouille—leftover ratatouille is great with grilled steak or burgers or with cold poached salmon. Add it to green salads or serve it on crackers or in sandwiches.

OLD-FASHIONED LEMON PUDDING WITH SEASONAL BERRIES

Homemade pudding makes a lovely warm-weather dessert, particularly because it can be refrigerated until time to serve. Serve this pudding the day it is made for the best flavor and texture.

$^{1}/_{4}$ *cup cornstarch*
$2^{1}/_{2}$ *cups milk*
3 large egg yolks
1 cup sugar
2 teaspoons finely grated lemon zest
$^{1}/_{8}$ *teaspoon salt*
$^{1}/_{2}$ *cup fresh lemon juice*
1 tablespoon pure vanilla extract
$^{1}/_{2}$ *cup heavy cream*
2 cups fresh blueberries, blackberries or sliced strawberries

1. In a saucepan, combine the cornstarch and $^{1}/_{3}$ cup of the milk and whisk until smooth. Add the egg yolks, sugar, 1 teaspoon of the zest and salt and whisk again. Stir in the remaining milk and cook over medium-low heat, whisking, for 4 to 6 minutes or until heated through. Raise the heat to medium-high and cook, whisking constantly for 3 to 5 minutes, until the mixture is boiling and smooth. It may first thicken and then thin out a little.

2. Strain the pudding mixture through a fine-meshed sieve into a bowl. Stir in the remaining zest and the lemon juice and set the bowl over a larger bowl filled with ice cubes and cold water. Let cool for 5 to 10 minutes, stirring occasionally, until the pudding starts to thicken. Stir in the vanilla extract.

3. In an electric mixer set on high speed, whip the cream to soft peaks and then fold into the pudding mixture. Spoon into six 6-ounce custard cups, cover with plastic wrap and chill for at least 1 hour before serving. Top with berries.

Serves 6

A Late Summer Lunch

ROASTED RED PEPPER SPREAD

When served with crisp raw vegetables, this spread might more appropriately be called a dip. But we adore it spread on Parmesan Garlic Toasts, too. The flavors mellow if this is made a day ahead of time.

2 red peppers, halved, seeded and deveined
1 tablespoon olive oil
$^1/_2$ pound cream cheese
$^1/_4$ cup sour cream
$^1/_2$ red onion, coarsely chopped
4 drops Tabasco sauce
$^1/_4$ teaspoon Worcestershire sauce
Pinch of cayenne pepper
2 tablespoons finely chopped chives
Assorted raw vegetables, Parmesan Garlic Toasts (see page 79) or crackers

1. Preheat the broiler. Place the pepper halves directly on a broiler tray pan and spoon the olive oil over them. Broil, turning often, until the skins are charred. Transfer to a small paper bag and fold to seal. Set aside to cool inside the bag. When cool, rub the charred skin from the peppers and cut them into fine dice. Transfer to a bowl.

2. Put the cream cheese, sour cream, onion, Tabasco sauce, Worcestershire sauce and cayenne in the bowl of a food processor fitted with the plastic or metal blade and process until smooth. Scrape the mixture into the bowl with the peppers. Add the chives and mix well. Cover and refrigerate for at least 1 hour.

3. Let the spread come to room temperature before serving. Serve with raw vegetables, Parmesan Garlic Toasts or crackers.

Serves 6; makes 1$^1/_2$ cups

MENU

ROASTED RED PEPPER
SPREAD

PENNE WITH GRILLED
SHRIMP, ASPARAGUS
AND PINE NUTS

SALAD OF TOMATOES,
CAPERS, RADICCHIO
AND ARUGULA

BLACKBERRIES IN
CASSIS WITH
MASCARPONE CREAM

PENNE WITH GRILLED SHRIMP, ASPARAGUS AND PINE NUTS

This is a light combination of penne, fresh asparagus, and grilled shrimp. Toss everything together just before serving and top with toasted pine nuts.

¼ cup plus 2 tablespoons extra-virgin olive oil
2 cloves garlic, thinly sliced
1 tablespoon chopped fresh rosemary
2 tablespoons dry white wine
1 tablespoon balsamic vinegar
Salt and freshly ground black pepper, to taste
1 pound large shrimp, peeled and deveined
1 pound fresh asparagus, trimmed and cut into 1-inch pieces
1 pound penne pasta
2 tablespoons fresh lemon juice
3 tablespoons freshly grated Parmesan cheese,
  plus more for garnish
½ cup toasted pine nuts (see Note)
Lemon wedges, for garnish

1. In a large glass or ceramic bowl, mix the olive oil, garlic, rosemary, wine, vinegar and salt and pepper and whisk.
2. Rinse the shrimp and pat them dry. Add them to the bowl and stir them gently with the marinade to coat. Cover and refrigerate for about 1 hour, stirring occasionally.
3. Preheat the broiler.
4. About 10 minutes before serving, bring a saucepan of boiling salted water to a boil and cook the asparagus for about 5 minutes until crisp-tender. Drain and set aside.
5. Remove the shrimp from the marinade, arrange on an aluminum foil–lined broiler tray and broil for about 6 minutes, turning the shrimp once during cooking, until pink. Set aside.
6. Meanwhile, bring a large pot of salted water to a boil and cook the pasta for about 8 minutes or until al dente. Drain and return to the

pot. Add the lemon juice and 3 tablespoons of cheese and toss well.
Add the shrimp, asparagus and pine nuts and toss again. Season to
taste with salt and pepper. Serve in shallow pasta bowls, sprinkled
with more cheese and garnished with lemon wedges.

Note: To toast the pine nuts, spread them in a shallow pan and roast in
a 350°F. oven or toaster oven for 3 to 5 minutes until golden and fragrant. Immediately transfer to a plate to stop the cooking and cool.
You may do this just before using, but because the broiler is being
used to cook the shrimp, it may be more convenient to toast the pine
nuts ahead of time.

Serves 6

SALAD OF TOMATOES, CAPERS, RADICCHIO AND ARUGULA

This is a delicious salad to serve when summer tomatoes are at
their peak.

2 tablespoons olive oil
6 cloves garlic, thinly sliced
3 red onions, cut into ¹/₂-inch dice
Salt and freshly ground black pepper, to taste
8 tomatoes, cut into ¹/₂-inch dice
1 teaspoon balsamic vinegar
2 teaspoons drained capers
1 large or 2 small bunches arugula, stemmed
1 head radicchio

1. In a skillet, heat the olive oil over medium heat. Add the garlic and onions and cook, stirring, for about 10 minutes, until translucent. Season with salt and pepper and set aside.

2. Put the chopped tomatoes in a large bowl. Add the vinegar and capers and toss. Add the cooked garlic and onions and toss again.

3. To serve, toss the arugula and radicchio together and arrange on individual salad plates. Top the lettuces with the tomato mixture.

Serves 6

BLACKBERRIES IN CASSIS WITH MASCARPONE CREAM

Make the most of beautiful blackberries' short season by serving them lightly sweetened and topped with rich mascarpone cream. If blackberries are in short supply, substitute another fresh berry. This is very nice accompanied by biscotti or another type of cookie.

MASCARPONE CREAM:
$\frac{1}{3}$ cup mascarpone cheese
1 tablespoon sugar
$\frac{1}{2}$ teaspoon pure vanilla extract
$\frac{2}{3}$ cup nonfat plain yogurt

BLACKBERRIES IN CASSIS:
4 cups fresh blackberries
$\frac{1}{4}$ cup crème de cassis
2 tablespoons sugar
1 tablespoon fresh lemon juice

1. To prepare the mascarpone cream, whisk together the mascarpone cheese, sugar and vanilla. Add the yogurt and stir until smooth. Cover and refrigerate for at least 1 hour.

2. To prepare the blackberries, put the berries in a large bowl. Add the crème de cassis, sugar and lemon juice and stir gently but thoroughly. If not serving immediately, cover and refrigerate for up to 1 hour.

3. Spoon the berries into goblets or decorative glass dessert bowls and top with the chilled cream. Serve immediately.

Note: The mascarpone cream can be made up to 2 days ahead and stored covered in the refrigerator.

Serves 6

PANTRY SUGGESTIONS

Roasted Red Pepper Spread—this can be made ahead of time and will keep for up to 4 days in the refrigerator. Use it spread on sandwiches, crackers or cocktail bread.

Penne with Grilled Shrimp, Asparagus and Pine Nuts—marinate some extra shrimp to thread on skewers, grill and serve as a first course or light meal. However, do not hold marinated shrimp in the refrigerator for more than 2 or 3 hours or they will turn soft and cottony. Use the same marinade later in the week with fresh shrimp.

Salad of Tomatoes, Capers, Radicchio and Arugula—make extra amounts of the tomato and caper mixture and spoon it over grilled chicken or fish, onto sandwiches or spoon it over other greens or cold, grilled vegetables.

Blackberries in Cassis with Mascarpone Cream—the cream is great over other berries, sliced peaches or nectarines or spooned on warm fruit pies or cobblers.

AUTUMN DINNERS

All human history attests
That happiness for man—the hungry sinner—
Since Eve ate apples, much depends on dinner.

LORD BYRON
1788–1824

A Delicious Pasta Dinner

SALAD OF MIXED GREENS, ROASTED PORTOBELLO MUSHROOMS AND RED ONIONS WITH SHERRY VINAIGRETTE

When autumn arrives, green salads tend to be more assertive. This one, composed of roasted vegetables and a boldly flavored vinaigrette, is just right before the pasta main course. Use other vegetables, if you prefer, such as roasted beets, eggplant or potatoes.

VINAIGRETTE:
1 tablespoon Dijon mustard
$^{1}/_{4}$ cup sherry wine vinegar
Salt and freshly ground black pepper, to taste
Pinch of dried tarragon
$^{3}/_{4}$ cup extra-virgin olive oil

SALAD:
8 large portobello mushrooms, cut into $^{1}/_{4}$-inch-wide slices
4 tablespoons olive oil
4 red onions, peeled, halved and cut into $^{1}/_{4}$-inch-wide slices
Salt and freshly ground black pepper
6 cups torn salad greens, such as mesclun mix, red leaf lettuce, Boston lettuce,
*   Bibb lettuce or green leaf lettuce (see Note)*
Shaved Parmesan or pecorino cheese, for garnish

1. To prepare the vinaigrette, combine the mustard and vinegar in a small bowl and whisk well. Season to taste with salt, pepper and tarragon and whisk again. Slowly add the olive oil, pouring it in a steady stream while whisking constantly to emulsify the vinaigrette. Taste and correct the seasoning, if necessary. Set aside until ready to use.

2. Preheat the oven to 350°F.

3. To prepare the salad, place the mushrooms in a shallow baking dish lined with aluminum foil, sprinkle with 2 tablespoons of the oil and season to taste with salt and pepper. Toss gently.

4. Spread the onions in another foil-lined baking dish, sprinkle with the remaining 2 tablespoons of oil and season to taste with salt and pepper. Toss gently.

5. Roast the mushrooms and onions for about 1 hour, until very tender. Stir them a few times during roasting. Set aside to cool.

6. To serve, put the greens in a large bowl and toss with about 2 tablespoons of the vinaigrette and then arrange on 6 salad plates.

7. Put the mushrooms in the bowl and toss with about 2 more tablespoons of the vinaigrette. Spoon these over the greens. Put the onions in the bowl and toss with about 1 tablespoon of the vinaigrette. Spoon these over the mushrooms. Top each salad with the shaved cheese and season with freshly ground pepper. Serve immediately.

Note: Use the freshest salad greens available. Many supermarkets and green grocers sell mesclun mix, a mixture of specialty lettuces, which adds lovely flavor, texture and color to any salad. Mix it with other soft, buttery greens.

Serves 6

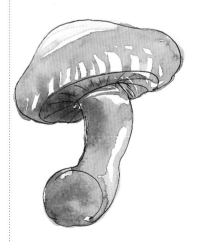

53

Farfalle with Tomato and Vegetable Sauce

It's hard to believe how simple this sauce is to make—all you need is about an hour and a few staples, including a large can of tomatoes. When a little heavy cream is swirled into the sauce just before serving, it is truly sublime, although it is still very good without it.

1 tablespoon olive oil
1 small onion, finely chopped
2 stalks celery, cut into $\frac{1}{2}$-inch slices
2 carrots, cut into $\frac{1}{2}$-inch rounds
1 can (28 ounces) whole tomatoes, with the juice
Salt and freshly ground black pepper, to taste
$\frac{1}{4}$ teaspoon sugar
1 pound farfalle or bow-tie pasta
$\frac{1}{4}$ cup heavy cream (optional)
6 tablespoons chopped fresh parsley, for garnish
Freshly grated Parmesan cheese, for garnish

1. In a large sauté pan, heat the oil over medium heat. Add the onion, celery and carrots and cook for about 10 minutes, stirring, until the vegetables begin to soften.
2. Add the tomatoes and their juice, raise the heat and bring to a boil. Season with salt and pepper. Stir in the sugar. Reduce the heat to medium-low and simmer, uncovered, for about 1 hour, stirring occasionally with a wooden spoon, until quite thick. Cool slightly.
3. Transfer the sauce to a food processor and process until smooth. This may have to be done in batches. Return the puréed sauce to the pan. (At this point, the sauce may be refrigerated or frozen.)
4. Meanwhile, bring a large pot of lightly salted water to a boil over high heat. Cook the pasta for 8 to 10 minutes or just until al dente. Drain and return to the pot. Cover to keep hot.
5. Heat the sauce over medium heat until simmering. Add the cream, if using, and stir for about 1 minute, until blended.
6. Spoon the pasta into 6 pasta or soup bowls and spoon the sauce over it. Garnish with fresh parsley and serve with the cheese.

Note: You can double the sauce recipe (omitting the cream) and freeze the excess for later use (see step 3).

Serves 6

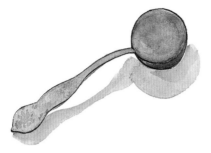

SOURDOUGH GARLIC BREAD

This garlic bread is equally delicious with either plain French bread or sourdough. Sourdough is chewier and its subtle tang blends seductively with the oil, garlic and cheese.

1 large sourdough baguette, halved lengthwise
4 to 6 large cloves garlic, halved
4 to 6 tablespoons olive oil
3 tablespoons freshly grated Parmesan cheese

1. Preheat the oven to 350°F.
2. Cut the baguette halves into thirds for 6 large pieces of bread. Rub each generously with garlic and then brush with olive oil. Sprinkle with cheese. Transfer to a baking sheet and bake for 15 to 20 minutes, until lightly browned. Serve hot.

Serves 6

RED BARTLETT PEAR TART

Pears are as much a part of autumn as pumpkins and scarlet foliage. This lovely tart is elegant in its simplicity, and pretty, too. A perfect ending to a relaxed Sunday meal, one of the nicest things about this tart is that it can be made a few hours before serving.

PASTRY DOUGH:
1 3/4 cups unbleached all-purpose flour
1 teaspoon salt
10 tablespoons (1 1/4 sticks) unsalted butter, chilled
1 tablespoon vegetable shortening, chilled
5 to 8 tablespoons ice water

PEAR FILLING:
4 to 5 red Bartlett pears, peeled, cored and thinly sliced
3 tablespoons fresh lemon juice
3 tablespoons sugar
1 tablespoon cornstarch
1/2 teaspoon grated nutmeg
3/4 cup seedless raspberry jam or currant jelly

1. To make the pastry dough: Put the flour and salt in the bowl of a food processor. Cut the chilled butter and shortening into pieces and add them to the food processor.

2. Pulse the food processor 4 to 5 times to break up the fat. With the the machine running, add 5 tablespoons of the ice water. Turn the food processor off and then pulse it 5 or 6 times. The dough should begin to mass on the blade. If not, add another tablespoon of water, or more as needed. When the dough holds together in a cohesive mass, it is done; do not overmix.

3. Turn the dough out onto the countertop. Flatten it with the palm of your hand, dust it lightly with flour, and wrap the dough in plastic wrap or waxed paper. Chill for 1 or 2 hours.

4. Preheat the oven to 350°F.

5. On a lightly floured work surface, roll the dough into a large rectangle, approximately 10-by-14 inches. Press the dough into an 8-by-11-inch tart pan. Trim the excess dough and crimp the edges.

6. Arrange the pears in 3 rows over the dough to fill the pan in a single layer. Sprinkle with the lemon juice.

7. In a small bowl, combine the sugar, cornstarch and nutmeg and mix well. Sift evenly over the pears. Bake for about 1 hour, or until the crust is golden brown and the filling is bubbling gently. Set on a wire rack to cool slightly.

8. In a small saucepan, heat the jam over medium-low heat until liquefied.

9. Loosen the edges of the tart and slide it onto a serving platter. Spoon the jam over the tart and let cool before serving.

Serves 6 to 8

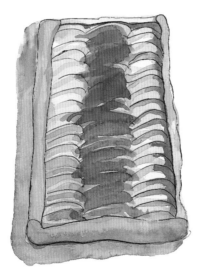

PANTRY SUGGESTIONS

Salad of Mixed Greens, Roasted Portobello Mushrooms and Red Onions with Sherry Vinaigrette—the vinaigrette can be used on any tossed green salad, as well as on warm boiled potatoes or macaroni for potato or pasta salads. Roast extra mushrooms and onions to eat at room temperature later in the week with grilled chicken or fish, or put the vegetables on sandwiches. The roasted vegetables are also good tossed with hot pasta, a little olive oil and minced garlic.

Farfalle with Tomato and Vegetable Sauce—the sauce is good on any sort of pasta, particularly cheese-filled ravioli or tortellini, although we also like it on strand pasta. It's good, too, spooned over sausage sandwiches. Stir canned lentils or thawed frozen lima beans or peas into the sauce to make it more filling and substantial.

Sourdough Garlic Bread—let the garlic bread sit out at room temperature for a day and then cut it into cubes to use as croutons in salads or soups or as part of a simple bread stuffing for poultry.

A Cold Weather Comfort Dinner

SALAD OF SMOKED SALMON, CUCUMBER, ENDIVE AND FENNEL WITH LEMON-DILL VINAIGRETTE

Topped with pale pink smoked salmon and garnished with feathery dill, this salad is a jumble of color, texture and flavor.

VINAIGRETTE:

3 tablespoons distilled white vinegar

2 teaspoons fresh lemon juice

½ cup extra-virgin olive oil

Salt and freshly ground black pepper, to taste

SALAD:

3 small cucumbers, peeled and cut into 1-inch-thick slices

4 endive, trimmed and cut into 1½-inch pieces

1 bulb fennel, trimmed, quartered and cut into 2-inch pieces

2 tablespoons finely chopped fresh dill

6 ounces smoked salmon, cut into bite-sized pieces

6 sprigs dill, for garnish

1. To prepare the vinaigrette, combine the vinegar and lemon juice in a small bowl and whisk well. Slowly add the olive oil, pouring it in a steady stream while whisking constantly to emulsify the vinaigrette. Season with salt and pepper and whisk again.

2. To prepare the salad, combine the cucumbers, endive and fennel in a large bowl and toss gently. Spoon about three-quarters of the vinaigrette over the vegetables and toss to mix. Add the chopped dill and toss again. Set aside.

3. Arrange the salad on 6 salad plates and top each with salmon. Drizzle the remaining dressing over the salmon, garnish with dill sprigs and season with more freshly ground black pepper.

Serves 6

BRAISED LAMB SHANKS WITH WHITE BEANS

Brisk weather demands hearty country food and these braised lamb shanks nicely fit the bill. The primary ingredients are simple, inexpensive fare but the array of spices renders this dish anything but ordinary, although the lengthy cooking subdues their flavors so that they accent in subtle ways. Both the shanks and the beans require time to marinate or soak, so plan accordingly, beginning your preparations on Saturday for a warm and comforting Sunday dinner.

MARINADE:
4 cloves garlic, thinly sliced
3 tablespoons olive oil
Salt and freshly ground black pepper

LAMB:
4 lamb shanks (about 6 pounds)
1/2 pound dried cannellini beans
1 onion, quartered
Salt and freshly ground black pepper
1 tablespoon olive oil
1 red onion, sliced
1 tablespoon ground cumin
1 teaspoon ground cinnamon
1 teaspoon ground coriander
1 teaspoon ground turmeric
1 teaspoon paprika
1/2 teaspoon cayenne pepper
4 carrots, sliced crosswise into 1-inch-thick pieces
1 1/2 cups dry red wine
1/2 cup beef stock
1 cup chopped canned tomatoes, with their juice
3/4 cup fresh bread crumbs
1 tablespoon unsalted butter
1 cup chopped fresh flat-leaf parsley

1. To prepare the marinade, combine the garlic, olive oil, salt and pepper in a small bowl and whisk to mix. Lay the shanks in a shallow glass or ceramic baking dish and pour the olive oil mixture over them. Cover and refrigerate for at least 8 hours and up to 24 hours, turning several times.

2. To prepare the beans, put the beans in a bowl and add enough cold water to cover by 1 to 2 inches. Cover and set aside to soak for at least 4 to 6 hours.

3. Drain and rinse the beans, transfer to a large saucepan and add fresh water to cover by 1 to 2 inches. Add the yellow onion and season with a little salt and pepper. Bring to a boil over high heat, reduce the heat and simmer for 45 minutes to 1 hour until the beans are tender but still offer some resistance. Drain and set aside.

4. In a large, deep skillet, heat the olive oil over medium-high heat. Remove the shanks from the marinade and cook, turning, until browned on all sides. Remove the shanks from the pan and set aside. Drain nearly all the fat from the pan.

5. Add the red onion slices to the pan and cook for about 5 minutes over medium heat, stirring gently, until soft. Stir in the spices. Add the carrots, wine, beef stock and tomatoes and bring to a boil over high heat. Reduce the heat to a simmer, add the shanks, cover and cook, stirring occasionally, for about 40 minutes.

6. Preheat the oven to 350°F.

7. Spoon half the beans into a large casserole and top with the shanks and vegetables. Spread the remaining beans on top, cover and bake for about 1 hour until the meat is tender.

8. Scatter the bread crumbs over the top of the casserole and dot with the butter. Bake, uncovered, for 25 to 30 minutes longer, or until the meat is very tender. Sprinkle with parsley and serve at once.

Serves 6

SAUTÉED CARROTS WITH BLACK OLIVES

Few recipes are easier to make than this one—it takes only minutes to cook. The pleasant saltiness of the olives blends nicely with the natural sweetness of the carrots, making this a piquant accompaniment to the mild lamb shanks.

1 tablespoon olive oil
1 pound carrots, sliced into 1-inch-thick rounds
2 tablespoons chicken stock, preferably homemade
2 tablespoons pitted and chopped salty black olives, such as niçoise,
  kalamata, or Gaeta

1. In a large sauté pan, heat the oil over medium-high heat. Add the carrots and cook for 5 to 7 minutes, tossing to coat with the oil, until the carrots are just tender.
2. Stir in the chicken stock, cover and cook for about 5 minutes until the carrots are tender. Stir in the olives and serve immediately.

Serves 6

BREAD PUDDING WITH RUM-RAISIN SAUCE

Homey bread pudding is the obvious ending to this meal of comfort food. You can use any good-quality bread, although we find baguette-style breads work best.

PUDDING:
½ cup (1 stick) unsalted butter, softened
Sixteen ½-inch-thick slices day-old French bread
3 large eggs
¾ cup plus 2 tablespoons sugar
4 cups milk
2 tablespoons pure vanilla extract
½ teaspoon ground nutmeg

PANTRY SUGGESTIONS

Salad of Smoked Salmon, Cucumber, Endive and Fennel with Lemon-Dill Vinaigrette—the vinaigrette is delicious over any green salad or steamed vegetables. Serve any leftover salmon on crackers or French bread as a before-dinner nibble with a glass of wine later in the week.

Braised Lamb Shanks with White Beans—leftover lamb shanks and white beans can be reheated gently, the meat cut from the bones, and served over thick slices of country-style bread for a weekday supper. Or, add a can of beef broth and another of plum tomatoes to the leftovers, heat through and serve as soup.

Bread Pudding with Rum-Raisin Sauce—if you make extra sauce, store it in the refrigerator for up to a week and pour it over ice cream, frozen yogurt or pound cake.

RUM-RAISIN SAUCE:

1 1/2 cups water

1/4 cup sugar

1/3 cup raisins

2 tablespoons unsalted butter

1 teaspoon unbleached all-purpose flour

1/4 cup dark rum

2 tablespoons fresh lemon juice

1. Preheat the oven to 325°F. Butter a large baking dish.

2. To prepare the pudding, generously butter the bread slices and arrange them buttered side up, in the baking dish in a single layer so that they cover the bottom of the dish.

3. In a large bowl, whisk the eggs with 3/4 cup of the sugar until smooth. Slowly add the milk, whisking constantly. Add the vanilla and nutmeg and whisk until mixed. Carefully pour the egg mixture over the bread and sprinkle with the remaining 2 tablespoons of sugar. Sprinkle a little more nutmeg over the top, if desired.

4. Put the baking dish in a larger roasting pan and add enough hot water to come halfway up the sides of the dish. Bake for 45 to 50 minutes, or until the custard is set.

5. To prepare the sauce, combine the water and sugar in a saucepan and bring to a boil over medium-high heat. Reduce the heat to medium, add the raisins and simmer for about 15 minutes to plump.

6. In a separate saucepan, melt the butter over medium heat. Add the flour and stir constantly until smooth. Slowly stir in the raisin mixture, and bring to a boil. Add the rum and lemon juice and cook, stirring, just until boiling. Remove from the heat.

7. Cut the pudding into squares and serve with the sauce spooned over the top.

Note: You can make the sauce ahead of time and warm it over low heat until hot, stirring well, just before serving.

Serves 10 to 12

An Autumn Harvest Dinner

ROASTED ACORN SQUASH SOUP

Acorn squash is an autumn treasure, its sweet, golden flesh, when roasted, can be transformed into a fragrant, creamy, smooth soup that gets a Sunday dinner off to a delicious start.

3 acorn squash, seeded and halved
4 carrots, cut crosswise into $1/2$-inch lengths
1 onion, quartered
1 tablespoon unsalted butter
1 tablespoon light brown sugar
4 cups chicken stock, preferably homemade
Salt and freshly ground black pepper, to taste
2 cups water
$1/2$ teaspoon ground ginger
Pinch of cayenne pepper
1 cup whole milk
2 tablespoons snipped fresh chives, for garnish

1. Preheat the oven to 375°F.
2. Put the squash halves, cut side up, in a large roasting pan and distribute the carrots and onions around them. Dot the vegetables with butter and sprinkle with brown sugar. Pour 1 cup of stock over the vegetables and season to taste with salt and pepper. Cover with aluminum foil and bake for about 1 hour, or until the squash is tender.
3. Let the squash cool in the pan until cool enough to handle. Scoop the squash flesh from the skins and transfer to a stockpot; discard the skins. Add the carrots, onions, any pan juices, the water and the remaining 3 cups of stock. Bring to a boil over high heat, reduce the heat to medium, stir in the ginger and cayenne pepper and simmer, uncovered, for about 20 minutes until the flavors blend.

MENU

ROASTED ACORN
SQUASH SOUP

QUICK BUTTERMILK
BISCUITS

ROASTED CORNISH
GAME HENS WITH
ORANGE SAUCE

SAUTÉED SPINACH
WITH RASPBERRY
VINEGAR

ORZO WITH
PORTOBELLO AND
CREMINI MUSHROOMS

PLUM COBBLER

4. Transfer the soup to a food processor or blender and puree until smooth. This will have to be done in batches. Return it to the pot. At this point, the soup can be refrigerated, covered, for 2 or 3 days or frozen for use later in the month.

5. Bring the soup to a gentle boil over medium-high heat. Add the milk, stir well, season to taste with salt and pepper and cook until piping hot. To serve, ladle into 6 soup bowls and garnish with the chives.

Serves 6

QUICK BUTTERMILK BISCUITS

Light, fluffy, steaming-hot biscuits are welcome at nearly any meal, but they seem especially appropriate for Sunday dinner. Pop these in the oven just before dinner so that they are fresh and hot at the right time.

2 cups unbleached all-purpose flour
1 tablespoon sugar
1 tablespoon baking powder
1 teaspoon salt
$\frac{1}{2}$ teaspoon baking soda
$\frac{1}{4}$ cup vegetable shortening, chilled
2 tablespoons unsalted butter, chilled
$\frac{2}{3}$ cup buttermilk
1 tablespoon finely chopped fresh rosemary (optional)
1 tablespoon finely chopped fresh chives (optional)
2 tablespoons unsalted butter, melted

1. Preheat the oven to 450°F.

2. Put the flour, sugar, baking powder, salt and baking soda into the bowl of a food processor and pulse briefly to mix. Add the shortening and butter and pulse 6 to 8 times until the mixture resembles coarse meal. Transfer to a bowl and blend in enough of the buttermilk to form a soft dough.

3. On a lightly floured work surface, knead the dough a few times until the dough holds together. Roll or pat the dough to a thickness of ¼ to ½ inch. Using 2- to 2½-inch round biscuit or cookie cutters or an upturned glass, cut biscuits and transfer to an ungreased baking sheet. Gather the scraps of dough, pat out again and cut more biscuits. Bake for 10 to 15 minutes until golden brown.

4. In a small bowl, stir the herbs, if using, into the melted butter and then brush the mixture over the hot biscuits. Serve immediately.

Makes about 12 biscuits

ROASTED CORNISH GAME HENS WITH ORANGE SAUCE

Tiny Cornish game hens make an elegant meal, and marinating them in a lively mixture of oranges, garlic and Madeira gives them an intense, fresh flavor.

CORNISH GAME HENS:
6 Cornish game hens, halved along the breastbone
   (approximately 1½ pounds each)
Juice of 1 large orange
2 tablespoons olive oil
3 cloves garlic, sliced
1 small onion, chopped
¼ cup Madeira
Salt and freshly ground black pepper
Zest of 1 orange, coarsely chopped into ¼-inch-long pieces

ORANGE SAUCE:
2 tablespoons Madeira
2 tablespoons chicken stock, preferably homemade
1 teaspoon sugar
1 tablespoon red wine vinegar

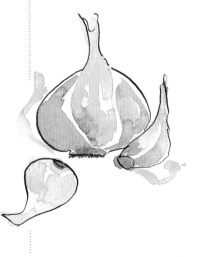

65

1. To prepare the hens, rinse the halves under cold running water and put them in a large glass or ceramic baking dish.

2. In a mixing bowl, combine the orange juice, oil, garlic, onion and Madeira, season to taste with salt and pepper and whisk well. Stir in the zest and then pour the marinade over the hens. Toss gently to coat, cover and refrigerate for at least 8 hours or overnight.

3. Preheat the oven to 450°F.

4. Transfer the game hens and the marinade to a large roasting pan and arrange in a single layer, skin side up. Roast for 30 minutes. Reduce the oven temperature to 350°F., baste and continue roasting for about 45 minutes or until the juices in the thighs run clear.

5. Remove the hens from the roasting pan and arrange on a large platter. Cover with aluminum foil and set aside to keep warm.

6. To prepare the sauce, strain the pan juices into a saucepan. Add the Madeira, stock, sugar and vinegar and stir well. Bring to a boil over high heat, reduce the heat to medium and simmer for 3 to 5 minutes or until slightly thickened and the flavors blend. Stir well to combine. Bring to a slow boil, reduce the heat and simmer for 3 to 5 minutes. Spoon the sauce over the hens and serve.

Serves 6

SAUTÉED SPINACH WITH RASPBERRY VINEGAR

Wilted spinach seasoned gently with just a splash of raspberry vinegar adds a welcome touch of green to the table.

2 tablespoons olive oil
3 cloves garlic, thinly sliced
2 large bunches (about 2 pounds) spinach, rinsed and stemmed
Salt and freshly ground black pepper, to taste
1 teaspoon raspberry vinegar

1. In a large sauté pan or skillet, heat the oil over medium-low heat and cook the garlic for 1 to 2 minutes, until tender. Add the spinach and cook, stirring and tossing occasionally, for about 2 minutes, until barely tender and wilted.

2. Season to taste with salt and pepper and then stir in the raspberry vinegar. Serve immediately.

Serves 6

ORZO WITH PORTOBELLO AND CREMINI MUSHROOMS

Specialty mushrooms, which are increasingly available in supermarkets as well as in gourmet shops and greengrocers, provide rich earthy flavors that seem particularly appropriate in the autumn. Here, we mix them with the tiny rice-shaped pasta called orzo.

1 tablespoon unsalted butter
1 tablespoon olive oil
2 large portobello mushrooms, cut into 1/4-inch slices
6 cremini mushrooms, cut into 1/4-inch slices
3 cups water
1 cup uncooked orzo
1/2 cup chopped flat-leaf parsley
1 tablespoon fresh lemon juice
Salt and freshly ground black pepper, to taste

1. In a large sauté pan, heat the butter and olive oil over medium heat until the butter melts. Add the portobello mushrooms and sauté for about 5 minutes. Add the cremini mushrooms and sauté for 7 to 10 minutes longer, until the mushrooms are nicely browned.

2. In a saucepan, combine the water and orzo and bring to a boil over medium-high heat. Reduce the heat to medium and cook for about 15 minutes or until the orzo is tender. Drain and return to the pan.

3. Stir in the mushrooms, parsley and lemon juice and season to taste with salt and pepper. Serve immediately.

Serves 6

PANTRY SUGGESTIONS

Roasted Acorn Squash Soup—make extra and freeze the soup for eating later in the month.

Quick Buttermilk Biscuits—split and toast these for breakfast served with butter and preserves. (These are best if not coated with herb butter.) Or serve left-over biscuits with sautéed mushrooms spooned over them.

Roasted Cornish Game Hens with Orange Sauce—the marinade is wonderful on chicken or duck, too. Make the sauce (without the pan juices it will be scant) and drizzle it on simple broiled or grilled chicken or veal cutlets. Use any leftover game hen meat to make a simple poultry salad mixed with orange vinaigrette, chopped scallions and orange

Orzo with Portobello and Cremini Mushrooms—sauté extra mushrooms and spoon over toast or biscuits for a light supper or lunch.

Plum Cobbler—turn the tables on the cobbler and use any leftover fruit filling as a warm topping for ice cream, frozen yogurt or plain butter cake or pound cake.

PLUM COBBLER

Small prune-plums, available from late summer through fall, are especially delicious in this cobbler. If you can't find them, use another larger plum. Be sure the plums are very ripe.

12 to 16 unpeeled prune plums, pitted and halved (about 1¾ pounds)
½ cup lightly packed light brown sugar
About 1 tablespoon fresh lemon juice
7 tablespoons unsalted butter, at room temperature
1 cup unbleached all-purpose flour
1 teaspoon baking powder
½ teaspoon salt
¼ teaspoon baking soda
¾ cup buttermilk
Whipped cream, for garnish (optional)

1. Preheat the oven to 425°F. Butter a 7-by-9-inch or oval 2 quart baking dish.
2. In a bowl, mix together the plums, sugar and lemon juice.
3. Spread the plum mixture and accumulated juices in the baking dish and make sure the plums are skin side up. Dot with 4 tablespoons of the butter. Bake, uncovered, for 25 minutes.
4. Just before the end of the baking time, combine the flour, baking powder, salt and baking soda and whisk 5 or 6 times. Add the remaining 3 tablespoons of butter and, using a pastry blender or fork, work in the butter until the mixture resembles coarse crumbs. Add the buttermilk, mixing quickly just until moistened. Remove the plums from the oven and spoon the flour mixture by large tablespoonfuls onto the plums. It will spread during baking. Return to the oven and bake for 15 to 20 minutes longer, or until the topping is lightly browned. Serve warm or at room temperature with whipped cream, if desired.

Serves 6

A Late Autumn Feast

SALAD OF ROASTED BEETS, ORANGES AND PECANS WITH TARRAGON VINAIGRETTE

As sweet-tasting as they are pretty to look at, roasted beets make a lovely autumn salad when combined with peppery arugula and juicy oranges.

3 pounds small beets (about 12 beets), scrubbed
3 tablespoons white vinegar
1 tablespoon fresh lemon juice
Salt and freshly ground black pepper
$1/2$ cup olive oil
1 teaspoon dried tarragon
1 bunch arugula, rinsed and stemmed
2 bunches watercress, rinsed and stemmed
2 navel oranges, peeled and cut crosswise into $1/4$-inch-thick slices
1 red onion, thinly sliced
$1/2$ cup pecan halves, lightly toasted (see Note)

1. Preheat the oven to 375°F.
2. Wrap 3 or 4 beets loosely in aluminum foil. Repeat with the remaining beets to make several packets and place on a baking sheet. Bake for about 1 hour, or until tender when pierced with a fork. Unwrap the beets and set aside to cool. Rub off the skins and cut into quarters. Cover and refrigerate for 3 hours or until cold (see Note).
3. Combine the vinegar, lemon juice, salt and pepper in a small bowl and whisk well. Slowly add the olive oil, pouring it in a steady stream while whisking constantly to emulsify the vinaigrette. Whisk in the tarragon, and taste and correct the seasoning, if necessary.
4. In a large bowl, toss the arugula and watercress with half the vinaigrette.

MENU

SALAD OF ROASTED
BEETS, ORANGES AND
PECANS WITH
TARRAGON
VINAIGRETTE

ROASTED DUCK WITH
PORT AND PLUM SAUCE

OVEN-BRAISED LEEKS
AND GARLIC

YUKON GOLD MASHED
POTATOES

BRANDIED PUMPKIN
TART WITH
GINGERSNAP CRUST

5. Arrange the greens on a large platter or on 6 salad plates. Top with the beets, oranges and red onion slices. Drizzle with the remaining vinaigrette and top with the toasted pecan halves. Serve immediately.

Note: The beets can be roasted up to 24 hours ahead and refrigerated.

To toast the pecans, spread them on a baking sheet and toast them in a preheated 350°F. oven or toaster oven for about 5 minutes until golden brown. Shake the pan once or twice for even toasting. Slide the nuts off the baking sheet to stop the cooking and let them cool.

Serves 6

ROASTED DUCK WITH PORT AND PLUM SAUCE

Delicious, crispy roasted duck is custom-made for a fall meal and because it pairs so naturally with fruit, the port and plum sauce is the ideal accompaniment. Instead of using fresh plums, we use Damson plum preserves for the richness they bring to the sauce.

One 5-pound duckling (labeled "ready to cook")
Salt and freshly ground black pepper
3 tablespoons fresh lemon juice
Grated lemon zest
1 tablespoon unsalted butter
1 cup peeled and finely chopped shallots (12 to 16 shallots)
1 tablespoon unbleached all-purpose flour
1 cup port
2 cups chicken stock, preferably homemade
½ cup Damson plum preserves

1. Preheat the oven to 425°F.
2. Remove and discard the duck giblets or reserve for another use. Rinse the duck and pat dry. Using a small sharp knife, prick the skin all over at ½-inch intervals. Season the duck's cavity with salt and pepper and lemon juice and place the zest inside. Tie the wings and legs

to the body with kitchen twine and close the cavity with small skewers. Place the duck, breast side up, on a rack in a roasting pan and roast for 30 minutes.

3. Reduce the oven temperature to 350°F., then turn the duck over and roast for 1 hour and 15 minutes, turning every 15 minutes, making sure it is on its back for the final 15 minutes of cooking. The duck is cooked when its thigh juices run clear when pricked with the tip of a knife. Remove from the oven and let stand for 10 minutes.

4. In a saucepan, melt the butter over medium heat, add the shallots and cook for 5 or 6 minutes until softened. Stir in the flour and cook, stirring, until well blended. Slowly add the port, stirring constantly, until it just comes to a boil. Add the chicken stock, stir well and bring to a boil. Reduce the heat to medium-low and simmer, uncovered, for about 30 minutes until the sauce is thickened and reduced by about half.

5. Strain the sauce through a sieve and return it to the saucepan. Add the preserves, stirring constantly with a wooden spoon, and cook over medium-low heat until the sauce is well blended, thickened and heated through.

6. Carve the duck and arrange it on a serving platter. Pass the sauce on the side.

Serves 6

OVEN-BRAISED LEEKS AND GARLIC

Leeks are one of the few vegetables that can be harvested from the late-fall garden, even after a frost, and as such they taste marvelously fresh at this time of year. Don't overlook this mild onion.

3 large leeks
2 tablespoons olive oil
6 cloves garlic, halved
3 or 4 tablespoons chicken stock, preferably homemade
Salt and freshly ground black pepper, to taste

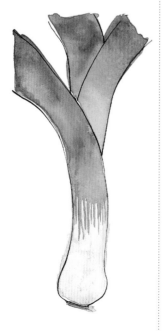

1. Preheat the oven to 350°F.

2. Trim the dark green tops and the root ends from the leeks. Cut the leeks in half lengthwise, rinse thoroughly and pat dry and then cut the halves crosswise into thirds.

3. Coat the bottom of a large baking dish with the olive oil and arrange the leeks and garlic halves in the dish. Drizzle 3 tablespoons of chicken stock over them and season to taste with salt and pepper.

4. Bake for about 45 minutes until the leeks are tender but still offering some resistance. Add a little more stock if the leeks seem dry and bake for 15 minutes longer until tender. Serve immediately.

Serves 6

YUKON GOLD MASHED POTATOES

Creamy Yukon Gold potatoes make smooth, full-bodied mashed potatoes—of course the butter and sour cream help a little, too.

6 Yukon Gold potatoes, peeled and cubed
1/2 cup milk, heated
1 tablespoon unsalted butter, at room temperature
1 tablespoon sour cream
Salt and freshly ground black pepper, to taste
2 tablespoons chopped fresh chives

1. Fill a large saucepan with lightly salted water and bring to a boil over high heat. Add the potatoes and return to a boil. Reduce the heat and simmer the potatoes for about 20 minutes until fork-tender. Drain and return the potatoes to the saucepan.

2. Using a hand-held electric mixer or a potato masher, begin mashing the potatoes. While mashing, add the milk, butter and sour cream. Season to taste with salt and pepper and mash until smooth.

3. Stir in the chives. Taste and correct the seasonings, if necessary, and serve at once.

Serves 6

BRANDIED PUMPKIN TART WITH GINGERSNAP CRUST

Even the kids at the table will love this luscious tart, despite the brandy. Serve with vanilla ice cream or whipped cream.

CRUST:
2 cups finely crushed gingersnap cookies (about 30 cookies)
1 tablespoon granulated sugar
4 tablespoons unsalted butter, melted

FILLING:
1 cup canned unsweetened pumpkin
$3/4$ cup evaporated milk
3 large eggs
1 cup lightly packed light brown sugar
1 teaspoon ground cinnamon
$1/2$ teaspoon ground ginger
$1/4$ teaspoon ground cloves
$1/2$ teaspoon ground nutmeg
$1/4$ cup brandy or cognac

1. Preheat the oven to 325°F. Generously butter a 10-inch glass or ceramic tart or pie pan.

2. To prepare the crust, in a bowl, toss the gingersnaps with the sugar. Pour in the butter and stir with a wooden spoon or work it in with your fingertips until the crumbs are moistened. Transfer to the tart pan and press evenly with the back of the wooden spoon or your fingertips to fit the pan. Bake for about 8 minutes, until very lightly browned. Cool completely on a wire rack.

3. To prepare the filling, in a mixing bowl, combine the pumpkin, evaporated milk and eggs and mix well with a spoon. Mix in the sugar, cinnamon, ginger, cloves and nutmeg. Add the brandy and mix thoroughly. Spoon the filling into the crust and spread it evenly.

4. Bake for 40 to 45 minutes until a knife inserted in the center comes out clean. Serve warm or cooled.

Serves 6 to 8

PANTRY SUGGESTIONS

Salad of Roasted Beets, Oranges and Pecans with Tarragon Vinaigrette—the roasted beets taste good mixed with roasted potatoes or onions, or tossed with a simple green salad. The vinaigrette is good tossed with roasted potatoes, another style of green salad or drizzled over broiled chicken.

Roasted Duck with Port and Plum Sauce—use the sauce with chicken or pork. Add it to a chicken or pork stir-fry in place of Asian plum sauce. Use leftover duck for a salad made with oranges and toasted pecans or walnuts, or toss it into a stir-fry made with red peppers, snow peas, and scallions and served over rice.

Oven-Braised Leeks and Garlic—chop leftover leeks and stir them into leftover mashed potatoes. Heat and serve as a substantial side dish or form the mixture into patties and pan-fry. Serve with fish or chicken.

Yukon Gold Mashed Potatoes—form leftover mashed potatoes into patties, pan-fry, and serve with scrambled eggs or omelets. If they seem too moist, add some bread crumbs.

Brandied Pumpkin Tart with Gingersnap Crust—the gingersnap crust is great with sweet potato pie, pecan pie or another pumpkin pie filling. This recipe can also be made into individual tartlets, which are great for after-school or late-night snacks.

WINTER DINNERS

Of all the days that's in the week
I dearly love but one day,
And that's the day that comes betwixt
A Saturday and Monday.

HENRY CAREY
1663–1743

A Savory Risotto Dinner

∾

MENU

∾

RISOTTO
WITH PORCINI
AND PORTOBELLO
MUSHROOMS
AND RED WINE

SALAD OF FENNEL
AND ARUGULA WITH
HONEY-MUSTARD
VINAIGRETTE

PARMESAN GARLIC
TOASTS

WALNUT CAKE WITH
SAUTÉED PEARS AND
CINNAMON CREAM

RISOTTO WITH PORCINI AND PORTOBELLO MUSHROOMS AND RED WINE

Risotto, a treasured dish in northern Italy, has garnered deserved attention in this country in recent years. The secret to creamy, perfect risotto is to use the right kind of rice and to stir diligently while adding the simmering stock. Be sure to have all of the ingredients ready before you start so that you can devote your time to tending the rice, which requires at least 15 minutes at the stove.

1 cup (4 ounces) dried porcini mushrooms
3 tablespoons olive oil
1 pound portobello mushrooms, sliced
  (about 4 large mushrooms)
2 cloves garlic, sliced
$1/2$ cup chopped flat-leaf parsley
2 tablespoons fresh lemon juice
Salt and freshly ground black pepper
1 quart chicken stock, preferably homemade
5 tablespoons unsalted butter
1 red onion, diced
$1^1/2$ cups uncooked arborio rice
$1/2$ cup dry red wine
$1/2$ cup freshly grated Parmesan cheese, plus more for garnish

1. Soak the porcini mushrooms in 1 cup of warm water for 15 to 20 minutes to plump. Remove the mushrooms from the soaking liquid and set aside. Strain the liquid through a sieve lined with cheesecloth and set aside.

2. Heat the olive oil in a large sauté pan over medium heat and sauté the portobello mushrooms for about 15 minutes until they begin to soften. Add the garlic and porcini mushrooms and cook for 3 or 4 minutes to soften the garlic. Add half of the soaking liquid and cook for about 10 minutes, or until the liquid is reduced to about 1 tablespoon. Add the parsley and lemon juice, season to taste with salt and pepper and stir to combine. Set aside to keep warm (see Note).

3. In a saucepan, bring the chicken stock to a boil over high heat. Reduce the heat and simmer while making the risotto.

4. In a large saucepan or stockpot, melt 4 tablespoons of the butter over medium heat and sauté the onion for about 5 minutes, just until softened. Remove the pan from the heat and add the rice, stirring until it is coated with butter. Return to the heat and stir in the remaining mushroom soaking liquid. Add 2 ladlesful of hot stock (about $\frac{1}{2}$ cup), stirring constantly, until the rice absorbs nearly all of the liquid. Continue adding more simmering stock, a ladleful or two at a time, and not adding more stock until the previous amount is absorbed by the rice. When nearly all of the stock has been added, the risotto will be creamy but the individual grains will be slightly firm (al dente). When the risotto reaches this point, stop adding stock.

5. Add the remaining 1 tablespoon of butter and the wine, stirring until both are well absorbed. Add the warm mushroom mixture and the Parmesan and stir gently, being careful not to overmix.

6. Serve immediately in large pasta or soup bowls with additional Parmesan cheese grated over the top.

Note: To insure that the mushroom mixture stays warm, hold it in a 200°F. oven rather than covering it, particularly if the lid is not tight fitting or the kitchen is drafty.

Serves 6

SALAD OF FENNEL AND ARUGULA WITH HONEY-MUSTARD VINAIGRETTE

Dressed with a bold vinaigrette, full-flavored, slightly crunchy fennel and arugula hold their own even as they surrender to the sum total of the ingredients to make a salad that beautifully offsets the creamy risotto.

VINAIGRETTE:
3 tablespoons balsamic vinegar
2 teaspoons Dijon mustard
2 teaspoons honey
Salt and freshly ground black pepper
1/4 cup extra-virgin olive oil

SALAD:
1 small (about 1/2 pound) fennel bulb, trimmed and sliced
1 bunch arugula, stems trimmed
6 cups torn salad greens, such as mesclun mix, red leaf lettuce,
*   Boston lettuce, Bibb lettuce or green leaf lettuce*
Cracked black pepper

1. To make the vinaigrette, combine the vinegar, mustard and honey in a small bowl and whisk well. Season to taste with salt and pepper and whisk again. Slowly add the olive oil, pouring it in a steady stream while whisking constantly to emulsify the vinaigrette. Taste and correct the seasoning, if necessary. Set aside until ready to use.

2. In a bowl, toss the fennel and arugula together. Add about half of the vinaigrette and toss gently to mix well.

3. Put the salad greens in a large salad bowl and drizzle with the remaining vinaigrette, tossing just to coat. Spoon the fennel and arugula over the greens, season to taste with the cracked pepper and serve immediately.

Serves 6

Parmesan Garlic Toasts

Hot garlic toasts pulled from the oven when the cheese has melted and just turned golden brown are irresistible and perfect for rounding out this simple Sunday dinner where risotto is the star.

1 loaf French or Italian bread, cut into twelve 1-inch round slices
6 cloves garlic, halved
3 or 4 tablespoons extra-virgin olive oil
2 or 3 tablespoons freshly grated Parmesan cheese

1. Preheat the oven to 350°F.
2. Rub each slice of bread generously with a garlic half and place on a baking sheet.
3. Brush the olive oil over the bread slices. Sprinkle with the cheese and bake for 3 or 4 minutes until golden brown. Serve immediately.

Serves 6

Walnut Cake with Sautéed Pears and Cinnamon Cream

An easy cake to make, this is lovely topped with spice-scented sautéed pears and sweetened cinnamon-spiced whipped cream.

Cake:
1¼ cups unbleached all-purpose flour
1 teaspoon baking powder
Pinch of salt
½ cup (1 stick) unsalted butter, at room temperature, cut into pieces
1 cup sugar
2 large eggs, at room temperature, separated
½ cup milk
1 cup chopped walnuts
1 teaspoon pure vanilla extract

PANTRY SUGGESTIONS

Salad of Fennel and Arugula with Honey-Mustard Vinaigrette—drizzle extra vinaigrette over other salads, warm roasted potatoes, roasted vegetables or sandwiches. It's also good over pan-fried or broiled fish or chicken.

Parmesan Garlic Toasts—coarsely chop leftover toasts to use as croutons in salads or sprinkled on top of hot soup. Ground in a food processor or blender, these make good bread crumbs to sprinkle on casseroles, pasta or vegetables.

Walnut Cake with Sautéed Pears and Cinnamon Cream—on its own, the walnut cake is good for an afternoon snack or packed in a lunch sack. Serve it for afternoon tea, too. It keeps, covered, for up to 5 days. Toast slices and serve them topped with ice cream for a quick dessert. The pears are outstanding over ice cream, frozen yogurt or plain, store-bought pound cake. The cinnamon-flavored whipped cream is great spooned into coffee or over fresh fruit and warm fruit pie.

SAUTÉED PEARS:
2 tablespoons unsalted butter
6 small Bosc pears, cored, peeled and cut into ¼-inch pieces
2 tablespoons brown sugar
1 tablespoon ground cinnamon
1 teaspoon ground nutmeg
2 tablespoons fresh lemon juice

CREAM:
1 cup heavy cream
1 tablespoon sugar
1 teaspoon ground cinnamon

1. Preheat the oven to 350°F. Lightly butter and flour a 9-inch round cake pan and tap out the excess flour.

2. To prepare the cake, in a bowl, combine the flour, baking powder and salt and whisk 8 to 10 times until well mixed.

3. Using an electric mixer set on medium-high speed, cream the butter and sugar. Add the egg yolks and beat until smooth. Add the dry ingredients in 3 or 4 batches, alternating with the milk and ending with the dry ingredients. Stir well and fold in the nuts and vanilla.

4. Using an electric mixer set on medium-high speed, beat the egg whites until they hold stiff peaks. Fold the whites into the batter just until mixed. Spread the batter in the cake pan. Bake on the center oven rack for 35 to 40 minutes or until a toothpick inserted in the center comes out clean. Turn out onto a wire rack to cool.

5. To prepare the pears, in a sauté pan or skillet, melt the butter over medium-high heat and cook the pears, stirring, for about 5 minutes, or just until softened. Sprinkle with the sugar. Add the cinnamon, nutmeg and lemon juice and mix well. Cover to keep warm.

6. To make the cream, using an electric mixer set on medium-high speed, whip the cream and sugar until the cream is thick but not dry. Add the cinnamon and continue whipping until the cream is the desired consistency. Serve the cake topped with the pears and cream.

Serves 6 to 8

A Hearty Winter Dinner

BAKED HAM WITH MUSTARD-RUM GLAZE

Perfectly baked ham—sweet and deeply browned on the outside and tender and juicy on the inside—speaks eloquently of Sunday dinner. Few meats are easier and less worrisome to prepare. Serve this with a selection of the specialty mustards, hot, sweet and tart. There will be ample leftovers, which are great for sandwiches and salads.

One 5-pound cooked half ham, bone in, excess fat trimmed

MUSTARD GLAZE:
1 tablespoon Dijon mustard
1 tablespoon dark brown sugar
3 tablespoons dark rum

1. Preheat the oven to 325°F. Line a shallow roasting pan with aluminum foil and set a roasting rack in the pan.
2. Place the ham, fat side up, on the rack and using a sharp knife, score the fat in a criss-cross or diamond pattern. Insert a meat thermometer into the thickest part of the meat. Do not let the thermometer touch the ham bone. Bake for 1½ to 2 hours.
3. To make the glaze, whisk the mustard and sugar together in a small bowl. Stir in the rum, a tablespoon at a time, until well blended. Set aside.
4. About 30 minutes before the ham is done, brush it all over with the glaze. Continue baking, basting the ham 2 or 3 times, until it is heated all the way through and the meat thermometer registers 130°F. Let the ham stand for 10 to 15 minutes before carving and serving.

Serves 10 to 12

MENU

BAKED HAM WITH MUSTARD-RUM GLAZE

CORN, CARROT AND ROSEMARY PUDDING

SAUTÉED KALE, SPINACH AND COLLARD GREENS

CRANBERRY RELISH WITH BLOOD ORANGE JUICE AND DRIED CHERRIES

APPLE CRISP WITH TOASTED PECANS AND CORIANDER

CORN, CARROT AND ROSEMARY PUDDING

Corn pudding is reminiscent of old New England and as such is an ideal dish for serving up tradition on Sunday, particularly when served alongside baked ham. When grated carrots and fresh rosemary are introduced, the pudding becomes deliciously up-to-date.

2 carrots, finely grated
3 large eggs, lightly beaten
1 cup milk
1 cup heavy cream
¼ cup unsalted butter, melted
1 tablespoon unbleached all-purpose flour
1 tablespoon sugar
Salt and freshly ground black pepper to taste
2 cups fresh or frozen corn kernels (see Note)
1 tablespoon chopped fresh rosemary

1. Preheat the oven to 325°F. Butter an 11-by-6-by-2-inch baking dish and set aside.

2. In a large bowl, combine the carrots, eggs, milk, cream, butter, flour and sugar and stir to mix. Season to taste with salt and pepper. Gently stir in the corn and rosemary.

3. Transfer the mixture to the baking dish and set the dish in a larger roasting pan. Put the pans in the oven and add enough boiling water to the roasting pan to come halfway up the sides of the smaller dish. Bake for 50 to 60 minutes, or until browned and a knife inserted in the center comes out clean. Let the pudding stand for 10 to 15 minutes before serving.

Note: If possible use fresh corn for this recipe. For 2 cups, use 3 or 4 ears of corn, depending on their size. Cook the ears in boiling water for 3 or 4 minutes and when cool, scrape the kernels from the ears with a sharp knife. If using frozen corn, there is no need to cook the kernels.

Serves 6 to 8

SAUTÉED KALE, SPINACH AND COLLARD GREENS

Fresh greens, such as kale, spinach and collards, are among the treasures of the colder months. They tenaciously cling to life in late-fall gardens and are sold in leafy splendor in markets all winter. If you have never cooked them, you are in for a surprise. They are simple to prepare, requiring only a large pan and a few minutes over good heat to wilt, release their liquid, and turn a gorgeous dark green. If you have a pan large enough, cook all of the greens at once; if not, cook them in two or three batches. Keep in mind that fresh greens shrink considerably when cooked and therefore the mass you begin with may seem disproportionately large. It isn't.

2 tablespoons olive oil
Two 1-pound bunches spinach, cleaned and stemmed
Two 1-pound bunches collard greens, cleaned and stemmed
One 1-pound bunch green or purple kale, cleaned and stemmed
Salt and freshly ground black pepper to taste

1. In a large skillet, heat the oil over medium-high heat. Add as much spinach, collards and kale as will fit in the pan and cook, stirring, for about 5 minutes until the greens begin to wilt. Season to taste with salt and pepper and then lift the greens from the pan with tongs and set aside on a large plate or in a large bowl. Continue cooking the remaining greens, adding more oil to the pan if necessary. Combine each cooked batch with any preceding it and when all the greens are wilted, return them to the pan. Stir to mix the batches.
2. Cover the pan and steam the greens over medium-high heat for about 1 minute. Uncover and cook for a few minutes longer until any liquid evaporates. Adjust the seasonings with salt and pepper, toss, and serve immediately.

Note: Greens that have not been picked fresh from a garden may taste bitter. If you suspect the greens you are cooking are not fresh, plunge them in boiling water for about 1 minute before draining and sautéing. This will remove any bitterness.

The trickiest part of cooking greens is cleaning them. Fill a sink with cold water and soak the greens for several minutes, gently swirling them to remove all grit and sand. Rinse in a colander under gently running cold water and then break off the tough stems. There is no need to drain the greens once washed; just give them a good shake.

Serves 6 to 8

CRANBERRY RELISH WITH BLOOD ORANGE JUICE AND DRIED CHERRIES

Tart relishes are a wonderful surprise when served with sweet ham and corn pudding. In winters gone by, the Sunday table was festooned wirh bowls of brightly colored, bold flavored relishes. Nowadays, we don't have to preserve our summer gardens by putting up jars of relishes and jellies, but it's a lovely touch to make a fresh relish every now and then. Blood oranges have bright red flesh and wonderfully sweet-tart juice. They are available in the wintertime, sometimes by the name Maltese oranges.

12 ounces fresh cranberries, rinsed
⅔ cup sugar
⅓ cup water
⅔ cup fresh blood orange juice or any sweet orange juice
½ cup plus 2 tablespoons dried cherries
2 tablespoons Grand Marnier

1. In a heavy saucepan, combine the cranberries, sugar, water, and orange juice and bring to a boil over high heat. Reduce the heat and simmer gently for about 10 minutes until the cranberries begin to pop.
2. Remove from the heat and stir in the dried cherries and Grand Marnier. Cool, cover, and refrigerate for at least 1 hour and up to 1 week. Serve chilled.

Makes about 4 cups

Apple Crisp with Toasted Pecans and Coriander

Apple crisp is a singularly American dessert (although its roots are tangled with those of English fruit desserts). More humble than a pie and also far easier to make, crisps have all the warm, sweet goodness of the homiest of baked fruit desserts. The dash of ground coriander is a surprise in this version, adding a hint of sophistication to the crisp.

FILLING:
6 tart green apples, such as Granny Smith, peeled, cored,
  and coarsely chopped (approximately 2 pounds)
$1/2$ cup sugar
1 tablespoon fresh lemon juice
1 teaspoon ground cinnamon
$1/2$ teaspoon ground coriander
$1/8$ teaspoon ground cloves
$3/4$ cup whole pecans, lightly toasted (see Note)
2 tablespoons apple cider

TOPPING:
$1/2$ cup unbleached all-purpose flour
$1/2$ cup sugar
4 tablespoons ($1/2$ stick) unsalted butter, chilled and cut into pieces

Ice cream or whipped cream, optional

1. Preheat the oven to 350°F.
2. To prepare the filling, in a large bowl, combine the apples, sugar, lemon juice, cinnamon, coriander, cloves and pecans and toss to mix. Transfer to a 12-by-8-by-2-inch baking dish and sprinkle the cider over the fruit.
3. To prepare the topping, combine the flour and sugar in a bowl and whisk together. Using your fingers or a pastry blender, cut the butter into the flour mixture, working it until the mixture is crumbly.

PANTRY SUGGESTIONS

Baked Ham with Mustard-Rum Glaze—leftover ham is perfect for sandwiches and in salads. Ham is also delicious sliced thin and used to top crackers spread with cream cheese for hors d'oeuvres or as a snack. Slice it, wrap the slices in aluminum foil and freeze them for up to 1 month. Chop the frozen slices into pieces, let them thaw, and toss with pasta, peas, and a sprinkling of chopped mint or parsley. Cook the slices and serve with fried eggs or add to omelets. Fry some finely chopped ham in a little oil and use it to flavor wilted greens.

Be sure to utilize the ham bone by using it soon after cutting the meat from it or freezing it for up to 1 month. Do not strip it of all meat; a meaty bone adds the most flavor. Use it to flavor split pea soup or lentil soup.

Cranberry Relish with Blood Orange Juice and Dried Cherries—serve leftovers with cold turkey, grilled chicken or spread on sandwiches. Packed into small sterilized jars, the relish is a wonderful holiday gift. To sterilize screw-top jars, rinse them with boiling water and let them drain dry. Spoon the relish into the jars and screw the lid on tightly. The relish will keep in the jars for up to 1 week if refrigerated.

Sprinkle evenly over the fruit and bake for 40 to 50 minutes until the topping is lightly brown and the fruit is bubbling. Serve warm, topped with ice cream or whipped cream, if desired.

Note: To toast the pecans, spread them on a baking sheet and toast them in a preheated 350°F. oven or toaster oven for about 5 minutes until golden brown and fragrant. Shake the pan once or twice for even toasting. Slide the nuts off the baking sheet as soon as they reach the desired color to halt the cooking. Let them cool.

Serves 6 to 8

A Sumptuous Holiday Feast

❧

WILD MUSHROOM CONSOMMÉ

This dark, woodsy broth is a light and sophisticated prologue to a winter feast. It is best to make it at least a day ahead to give the mushrooms, vegetables and peppercorns time to steep so that the rich flavors infuse the broth.

1 pound shiitake mushrooms with stems, halved
½ pound white mushrooms, stemmed and halved
½ pound cremini mushrooms, stemmed and halved
1 white onion, coarsely chopped
2 carrots, coarsely chopped
1 rib celery, coarsely chopped
6 black peppercorns
6 green peppercorns
6 red peppercorns
½ cup chopped flat-leaf parsley
4 quarts water
Salt and freshly ground black pepper, to taste
4 white mushrooms, thinly sliced, for garnish
Lemon slices, for garnish
6 tablespoons snipped chives, for garnish

1. In a large nonreactive stockpot, combine the shiitake, white and cremini mushrooms, onion, carrots, celery, peppercorns and parsley with the water and season to taste with salt and pepper. Bring to a boil over medium-high heat. Reduce the heat, skim any foam that rises to the top, and simmer for 25 to 30 minutes until reduced by half. Set aside to cool and then cover and refrigerate for at least 8 hours or overnight.

2. Strain the soup through a fine sieve or a strainer lined with

MENU
❧
WILD MUSHROOM
CONSOMMÉ

FILLET OF BEEF

BROCCOLI PURÉE

MIXED VEGETABLES
AND FLAGEOLETS
WITH LEMON-HERB
VINAIGRETTE

CHOCOLATE CAKE
WITH CHOCOLATE
CREAM CHEESE
FROSTING AND
RASPBERRY SAUCE

cheesecloth. Discard the solids and return the broth to the pot and heat over medium-high heat until very hot. Adjust the seasonings with salt and pepper.

3. Ladle into soup bowls and garnish with the white mushroom slices, lemon slices and fresh chives. Serve immediately.

Note: Mushrooms absorb water and so should never be soaked in water or left under running water for more than a few seconds, if at all. In most cases, they can be cleaned simply by wiping with a damp cloth.

Serves 6

FILLET OF BEEF

Fillet of beef is always impressive, always elegant and so easy to prepare it leaves you time to enjoy a truly special Sunday dinner. Fillet is expensive, so take care when roasting, as nothing salvages overcooked meat. Use an accurate meat thermometer and keep a close eye on the meat. Hope for leftovers—fillet of beef is delicious cold and makes fabulously indulgent sandwiches.

One 4- to 5-pound beef fillet, trimmed and tied (see Note)
2 cloves garlic, halved
1 teaspoon olive oil
1 to 1½ teaspoons salt
Freshly ground black pepper, to taste

1. Preheat the oven to 450°F.

   2. Rub the meat with the garlic, brush it with the olive oil, sprinkle it with the salt and season it generously with pepper. Place on a roasting rack set in a shallow roasting pan. Roast for 10 minutes and then reduce the heat to 350°F. For rare, roast for 25 minutes longer or until a meat thermometer registers 120°F.; for medium, roast for 35 minutes longer or until a meat thermometer registers 130°F.

3. Let the roast stand for about 10 minutes to give the juices time to collect before slicing into ¾-inch slices. Serve immediately.

Note: Order fillet of beef from a reputable butcher. Ask for the meat to be trimmed and tied with butcher twine. If you live in an area with only a supermarket, ask the staff butcher to prepare the fillet for you.

Serves 6

BROCCOLI PURÉE

A mildly flavored purée complements the richness of the fillet of beef and its soft texture offsets the slight crunchiness of the mixed vegetables to round out a lovely meal.

2 pounds fresh broccoli, trimmed and separated into florets
1½ cups sour cream
1 teaspoon freshly grated nutmeg
Salt and freshly ground black pepper
2 tablespoons freshly grated Parmesan cheese

1. Preheat the oven to 350°F.
2. In a large saucepan, cook the broccoli in lightly salted boiling water over medium-high heat for 7 or 8 minutes or until fork-tender. Drain.
3. In a food processor, combine the broccoli, sour cream and nutmeg and process until smooth. Season to taste with salt and pepper and pulse to mix. Transfer to a casserole and sprinkle with the grated cheese. Cover and bake for 20 to 25 minutes or until hot. Serve immediately.

Serves 6

Mixed Vegetables and Flageolets with Lemon-Herb Vinaigrette

This dish can be served warm, at room temperature or even chilled, depending on your preference and your timetable. Tender, pale green flageolets are tiny French kidney beans, and since they are generally sold dried, they require overnight soaking. Here, their delicate flavor is accentuated by a lemony vinaigrette.

VEGETABLES:
1 pound dried flageolets
Salt
1 pound carrots, sliced into 1-inch rounds
2 fennel bulbs, tops removed, and quartered
2 tablespoons olive oil
1 pound haricots verts, trimmed
1 pound asparagus, trimmed

VINAIGRETTE:
1 cup extra-virgin olive oil
¼ cup red wine vinegar
2 tablespoons fresh lemon juice
2 tablespoons herbes de Provence, or a mixture of dried oregano,
  basil, rosemary, sage and thyme
Salt and freshly ground black pepper

1. To prepare the vegetables, in a bowl, combine the flageolets with enough water to cover by about 1 inch and set aside to soak for at least 6 hours or overnight.
2. Drain the flageolets and transfer them to a stockpot. Add enough water to cover, season with a little salt and bring to a boil over high heat. Reduce the heat and simmer, uncovered, for about 1 hour until just tender. Drain and set aside.
3. Preheat the oven to 350°F.
4. Put the carrots and fennel in a roasting pan. Add the olive oil, a little salt and mix well. Roast, uncovered, for about 1 hour until the veg-

etables are tender. Set aside to cool until warm or room temperature.

5. In a saucepan or deep skillet, cook the haricots verts for about 5 minutes until just tender. Drain and set aside until warm or room temperature, depending on preference. Repeat with the asparagus.

6. To prepare the vinaigrette, combine the olive oil, vinegar, lemon juice and herbs in a small bowl and whisk well. Season to taste with salt and pepper.

7. To serve, arrange the vegetables on a large platter. Whisk the vinaigrette and pour about half over the vegetables. Toss the flageolets with the remaining vinaigrette and season to taste with salt and pepper. Spoon the flageolets onto the platter with the vegetables and serve, or serve them in a separate bowl alongside the vegetables.

Serves 6

CHOCOLATE CAKE WITH CHOCOLATE CREAM CHEESE FROSTING AND RASPBERRY SAUCE

After a meal as elaborate as this one, nothing will do but an indulgent chocolate dessert, and this rich layer cake, coated with swirls of chocolate frosting and topped with raspberry sauce, deliciously fits the bill.

CAKE:
1 3/4 cups unbleached all-purpose flour
1 1/2 teaspoons baking soda
1/2 teaspoon baking powder
Pinch of salt
4 ounces unsweetened chocolate, coarsely chopped
1 cup (2 sticks) unsalted butter
1 cup hot water
2 cups sugar
2 large eggs, at room temperature
1 teaspoon pure vanilla extract

RASPBERRY SAUCE:

Two 10-ounce packages frozen raspberries in light syrup, partially thawed
1 tablespoon plus 1 teaspoon arrowroot
1 tablespoon orange juice, Grand Marnier or Cointreau

FROSTING:

12 ounces bittersweet chocolate, coarsely chopped
9 ounces cream cheese, softened
1 cup (2 sticks) unsalted butter, softened
1 cup confectioners' sugar
1 teaspoon pure vanilla extract

1. Preheat the oven to 350°F. Lightly butter and flour two 9-inch cake pans and tap out the excess flour (see Note).

2. To prepare the cake, in a bowl, combine the flour, baking soda, baking powder and salt and whisk 8 to 10 times until well mixed. Set aside.

3. In the top of a double boiler set over barely simmering water, combine the chocolate, butter and water and stir until the mixture is smooth and the chocolate is melted. Pour into a mixing bowl and stir in the sugar. Cool to lukewarm.

4. Using an electric mixer set on medium speed, beat the eggs, one at a time, into the batter until well mixed. Add the vanilla and beat just to mix. Gradually add the dry ingredients, mixing on low speed or stirring by hand, until the batter is smooth.

5. Divide the batter evenly between the pans and tap gently on the countertop to burst any air bubbles and distribute evenly. Bake on the center rack of the oven for about 30 minutes or until the center springs back when lightly touched and the edges of the cakes pull away from the sides of the pan. Cool the cakes in the pans set on wire racks for about 5 minutes and then turn out onto the racks to cool completely.

6. To prepare the raspberry sauce, drain the raspberries over a bowl and reserve the juice. Transfer the raspberries to a glass or ceramic bowl and set aside. Set aside 1 cup of the drained juice and discard the rest.

7. In a small cup, combine the arrowroot with 1 tablespoon of the reserved juice and stir until smooth. Pour this mixture into the remaining juice and transfer to a nonreactive saucepan. Bring to a boil over medium-high heat, stirring constantly, cooking for 30 to 60 seconds only. Remove from the heat and stir in the orange juice or liqueur.

8. Pour the heated sauce over the raspberries and stir gently until mixed. Cover and refrigerate for at least 1 hour until chilled. The sauce keeps covered and refrigerated for 2 days.

9. To make the frosting, in the top of a double boiler set over hot but not simmering water, melt the chocolate, stirring until smooth. Remove the top of the double boiler from the heat and let the chocolate cool for about 5 minutes until lukewarm.

10. Using an electric mixer set on medium-high speed, beat the cream cheese and butter until smooth. Add the sugar, about ¼ cup at a time, and beat for 1 or 2 minutes until smooth. Add the vanilla and melted chocolate and continue beating for about 1 minute until well mixed and fluffy. Set aside at room temperature until ready to use.

11. When cool, trim the cake layers so that they sit evenly on top of each other. Spread about ½ cup of the frosting over the bottom layer and set the top layer on it. Frost the sides and top of the cake generously. Serve with the chilled raspberry sauce passed on the side.

Note: If you take the extra step of lining the buttered and floured baking pans with waxed paper and then butter and flour the paper, the cake layers will be easier to remove from the pan. Once the cakes are removed from the pans, peel the waxed paper from the layers and let the cakes cool.

Serves 8 to 12

Recipe Index

TABLE OF EQUIVALENTS
The exact equivalents in the following tables have been rounded for convenience.

OVEN TEMPERATURES			WEIGHTS		LENGTH MEASURES		LIQUIDS		
Fahrenheit	*Celsius*	*Gas*	*US/UK*	*Metric*			*US*	*Metric*	*UK*
250	120	½	1 oz	30 g	⅛ in	3 mm	2tbl	30 ml	1 fl oz
275	140	1	2 oz	60 g	¼ in	6 mm	¼ cup	60 ml	2 fl oz
300	150	2	3 oz	90 g	½ in	12 mm	⅓ cup	80 ml	3 fl oz
325	160	3	4 oz (¼ lb)	125 g	1 in	2.5 cm	½ cup	125 ml	4 fl oz
350	180	4	5 oz (⅓ lb)	155 g	2 in	5 cm	⅔ cup	160 ml	5 fl oz
375	190	5	6 oz	185 g	3 in	7.5 cm	¾ cup	180 ml	6 fl oz
400	200	6	7 oz	220 g	4 in	10 cm	1 cup	250 ml	8 fl oz
425	220	7	8 oz (½ lb)	250 g	5 in	13 cm	1½ cup	375 ml	12 fl oz
450	230	8	10 oz	315 g	6 in	15 cm	2 cups	500 ml	16 fl oz
475	240	9	12 oz (¾ lb)	375 g	7 in	18 cm	4 cups/1qt	1l	32 fl oz
500	260	10	14 oz	440 g	8 in	20 cm			
			16 oz (1 lb)	500 g	9 in	23 cm			
			1½ lb	750 g	10 in	25 cm			
			2 lb	1 kg	11 in	28 cm			
			3 lb	1.5 kg	12 in	30 cm			